# DID YOU KNOW THIS ABOUT WORLD WAR II?

*The Most Interesting Trivia Book
About The Second World War*

War Trivia Unleashed Volume 1

**Bill O'Neill**

# DON'T FORGET YOUR
# FREE BOOKS

GET THEM FOR FREE ON
WWW.TRIVIABILL.COM

# CONTENTS

# CHAPTER 1:

# THE ROAD TO WAR

## IN THE UNITED STATES

### What Were the Results of the 1932 United States Presidential Election?

The 1932 U.S. presidential election pitted Democrat Party challenger, Franklin Delano Roosevelt, the Governor of New York, against incumbent President Herbert Hoover. Due to a number of factors, foremost was the Great Depression and Hoover's inability to do anything about it, Roosevelt won the election in an electoral and popular landslide. Roosevelt carried forty-two states and 472 electoral votes to only six states and fifty-nine electoral votes for Hoover. In the popular vote, Roosevelt won 57% of the electorate with 22,821,277 votes versus 15,761,254 votes for Hoover. During his record three plus terms as president, Roosevelt guided American domestic and foreign policy, assuming a strong stance against fascism in Europe.

### What was the German-American Bund?

The German-American Bund, often abbreviated as "Bund," was a fascist, pro-Nazi American political organization that was formed in 1936 with the blessing of the German National

Socialist German Worker's Party. The Bund was comprised of German immigrants and German-Americans, although some chapters also had Irish-American members. Its activities included holding rallies and marches, conducting training at paramilitary camps, and handing out propaganda on street corners. The government took a hardline against the group in the lead up to World War II and once the war began it was essentially proscribed. Other fascist groups, such as the Silver Shirts, attempted to fill the void but due to a combination of extreme government pressure and a lack of interest among Americans, the Bund's successors gained little traction.

## What Was Charles Lindbergh's Nickname?

American inventor, aviator, and activist Charles Lindbergh (1902-1974) became known as "Lucky Lindy" after he made the first solo flight across the Atlantic Ocean in 1927. The son of an influential Minnesota congressman, Lindbergh had the advantage of influential connections and a high IQ that helped him find success in nearly everything he did, which included engineering, inventing, aviation, and politics. In the years before World War II, Lindbergh gathered influential Americans from both the right and left wings of the political spectrum to form an organization known as the American First Committee to oppose American involvement in the war. After the Japanese attack on Pear Harbor, the Committee folded and Lindbergh served the American war cause by working with private aircraft contractors, eventually flying bombing raids in the Pacific as a civilian.

## What Were the Neutrality Acts?

After World War I and during the Great Depression, Americans had no desire to get entangled in another European war. Congress passed a series of laws that made it illegal for Americans to sell arms or give loans to any belligerents in the current war known as the Neutrality Acts. The Acts were slightly amended in 1937 to allow belligerents to buy American non-military materials with cash.

## How Did the Cash and Carry Policy Replace the Neutrality Acts?

After Germany invaded Poland in September 1939, some in the American government, including President Roosevelt, thought that something should be done to help those fighting the Axis powers, but the Neutrality Acts stood in the way. Congress passed a bill that was signed by the president on November 5, 1939 that allowed American companies to sell arms to belligerents in the war on a cash only basis. Since the British controlled the seas, it was all but assured that the only customers would be Allied nations. The Cash and Carry scheme then led to the Lend-Lease policy on March 11, 1941, which gave free food and other materials to the countries fighting the Axis powers.

# IN THE SOVIET UNION

## What Was Joseph Stalin's Birth Name?

Joseph Stalin's birthname was Ioseb Bsarionis dze Jughashvili. Stalin/Jughashvili was born on December 18, 1878 in the town of Gori in the country of Georgia. Although the town that Stalin was born in was majority ethnic Georgian, and Stalin was an ethnic Georgian, it was part of the Russian empire. As a young man Stalin became interested in Marxism and communism while he was at a seminary. He later moved to Russia, became active in communist politics, did time in a Siberian prison for his activities, and changed his name to the more Russian name "Stalin," which means "steel" in Russian.

After Vladimir Lenin died in 1924, Stalin became the leader of the Soviet Union until his death in 1953. Although remembered for leading his people against Germany in World War II, Stalin was also known for repression, atrocities, and genocide.

## What Impact Did the Great Purge Have on World War II?

Joseph Stalin is remembered as one of the most repressive dictators of the twentieth century. And for good reason. He instituted polices that resulted in genocide of non-Russian nationals in the U.S.S.R. and sent millions of dissenters to prison camps, known as *gulags*, where many of them died. Among the repressive tactics Stalin used on his opponents, perhaps none affected the Soviet Union's prospects in World War II more than the so-called "Great Purge." After Stalin's friend and personal doctor, Sergey Kirov, was assassinated, Stalin began a systematic purge of the Soviet Union and Communist Party that lasted until 1938. Nearly every member of the politburo and the surviving Bolsheviks from 1917 were executed, but more importantly about half of the generals of the Red Army were killed. Due to the loss of the officer corps, the Red Army performed quite poorly in the Winter War and the early stages of World War II. The situation was so bad that People's Commissar for Defense, Kliment Voroshilov, risked his life when he told Stalin, "You're the one who annihilated the Old Guard of the army; you had our best generals killed!"

## What Was the Holodomor?

The Holodomor was a manmade famine that took place in Ukraine during 1932 and 1933, resulting in the deaths of up to twelve million people. To many Ukrainians, the Holodomor is known as the "Ukrainian Genocide." The genocide was caused by a number of factors: the Soviets' drive to collectivize all farms, over optimistic harvest predictions, and a lack of support by the Soviet government once it began. There is little doubt among scholars that it was a manmade disaster and could have been avoided, but there is debate over whether or not Stalin purposely initiated policies that led to it and then aggravated its effects after it started. There is little doubt, though, that Stalin feared a Ukrainian independence movement and harbored resentment toward many non-Russian nationals. Stalin also viewed independent farm owners, whom the Communists called *kulaks*, as an enemy group. Holodomor means "death by hunger" in Ukrainian.

## How Did Stalin's Five Year Plans Limit the Soviet Union's Ability to Wage War?

After Joseph Stalin came to power, he eliminated Lenin's more liberal economic policies and in 1928 began instituting the centrally planned economic programs known as the "Five Year Plans." The idea of the Five Year Plans was to increase Soviet industrial output above that of Western nations and to collectivize all farms in the Soviet Union. Although industrial production was greatly increased throughout the nation, it was done so at the expense of agriculture. The forced collectivization program led to millions of deaths of otherwise healthy men who could have fought against Germany and the collective farms that were in operation on the eve of the German invasion in 1941 were woefully inefficient: agricultural production had yet to reach 1928 levels, which mean that the Red Army had difficulties feeding its troops.

## What Was the Red Army?

The Workers' and Peasants' Red Army, usually shortened to "Red Army," was the combined armed forces of the Union of

Soviet Socialist Republics (U.S.S.R.)/Soviet Union before and during World War II. After the Bolsheviks came to power in 1917, they wanted to eliminate all vestiges of tsarist Russia, which mean rapidly overhauling the existing, pro-tsar military. The Red Army was formed in 1918 as the military wing of the Communist Party and performed quite well in the Russian Civil War (1918-1922) due to its use of superior tactics and discipline. Under Lenin, Communist Russia was willing to allow officers who served under the tsars to continue to serve in the Red Army, but they were to be monitored by *commissars*. Commissars were ardent Communist Party ideologues who were assigned to units in order to monitor officers' loyalty to the cause. After the Communists won the Civil War and consolidated their hold over Russia, the commissars gained even more power over the Red Army, which led to operational and strategic problems in the early stages of World War II.

# IN GERMANY

## What Was the German Hyperinflation Cycle?

The German hyperinflation of 1921-1923 was when prices on commodities reached the 1,000% inflation mark, which separates normal inflation from hyperinflation. Germany's hyperinflation cycle was brought on by a number of factors: heavy war debts and reparations from World War I, a speculative crisis, French occupation of the mineral rich Ruhr region, and too much currency in circulation. The crisis ended when the Allied powers agreed to a new payment package with Germany and Germany in turn created a new currency, but the damage had been done. The Weimar government looked inept and weak to most Germans, who then began turning to far-right and far-left political organizations for answers.

## What Were the Freikorps?

The Freikorps, translated into English as "Free Corps," were German right-wing paramilitary squads largely comprised of World War I veterans. The Freikorps became particularly active during the German hyperinflation cycle of the early 1920s and the general political instability of that decade. The restrictions of the Versailles Treaty prevented Germany from having a large military, but provisions in it allowed veterans to keep their personal arms, which were utilized by different Freikorps groups. Although the Freikorps had no central authority and were essentially autonomous groups and cells, they shared a virulent anti-communist ideology that the Weimar government at times used to eliminate their enemies. With that said the Freikorps also generally detested the Weimar Republic. When the National Socialist German Worker's Party began to gain strength and grow in popularity, many Freikorps members joined, often swelling the ranks of local Storm Trooper contingents.

## What Was the Weimar Republic?

The Weimar Republic was the name of the German government from after World War I in 1918 until the National Socialists took power in 1933. The government was so named because the city of Weimar is where the constitution was drafted, but it was never known as such until years later. The Weimar Republic was different than previous and later forms of the German government because it was a semi-presidential system. In many ways, the Weimar Republic was marked by extremes: Germany, especially Berlin, became a center for new art movements and modern culture, but at the same time World War I veterans were having difficulties surviving. The Weimar Republic was for the most part inept in dealing with problems like the hyperinflation cycle and the

Great Depression, so the ranks of the National Socialist German Workers' Party and the Communist Party swelled.

## How Did the National Socialist German Workers' Party Form?

The Nationalsozialistche Deutsche Arbeitpartei (NSADP, often just abbreviated as Nazi), began in 1920 in the southern German province of Bavaria. It formed after Adolph Hitler and other World War I veterans joined the right-wing German Workers' Party in 1919, drafted a twenty-five-point statement of ideals, and changed the named to NSDAP. Like many fascist movements of the period, it incorporated some leftist ideas into its economic plan while placing racial and anti-Semitic philosophies in the vanguard. Although the NSDAP sought to take factory members and other union members away from the communist and socialist parties, it made minimal inroads in that respect: about 45% of its members were skilled workers and about 21% were white collar professionals.

## What Are the Origins of the Swastika?

"Swastika" is the ancient Sanskrit word for the symbol that has become synonymous with Nazi Germany. The earliest known swastikas were used in ancient Indian art as symbols of the sun, intended to bring fortune and power. Swastikas were also used, although with different names, in the art of ancient Greece, among the Norse, and in medieval Europe. Beside different Indo-European peoples, swastikas have been used in Japanese art and variants can even been seen in African and Native American art. In the early twentieth century, the swastika became a popular artistic motif in the West and can be seen on architectural designs from before World War II and was often used as decorations on sports teams' jerseys. The National Socialist Party adopted the swastika as their symbol in the early 1920s, which they referred to as the *Hakenkreuz* (crooked cross), for a number of reasons. First, they were utilizing the general popularity of the symbol at the time and second, they believed that since it was an ancient symbol of the Aryans it would tie their party to the glorious past of a lost age.

## What Was the *Sturmabteilung*?

The *Sturmabteilung* (SA), which translates from German into English as "Storm Detachment," was the paramilitary wing and street level fighters of the National Socialist Party before they took power. Often referred to as the "Storm Troopers," or "Brown Shirts" for the color of their uniforms, the SA provided protection for the Nazi Party leaders and engaged communists and other political enemies in street brawls. Formed in 1921, the SA's membership was much more proletarian than the majority of the party, with a majority being factory workers and tradesmen. The SA played a central role in Hitler's failed Munich Beerhall Putsch of 1923 and were one of the primary forces behind *Kristallnacht*. Fearing that the SA was getting too powerful, Hitler had the SA leadership arrested, including its commander Ernst Röhm, on the evening of June 30, 1934. Röhm was "allowed" to commit suicide and up to 200 other SA members were killed in a purge that became known as the "Night of the Long Knives." The SA was effectively sidelined with many of its remaining members being funneled into the SS or the regular military.

## How Did the Nazis Use the Idea of *Volksgemeinschaft*?

Volksgemeinschaft is a German word that basically translates into English as "people's group" or "people's community." It refers to the idea of one German people, regardless of class differences. The term and concept pre-dated Hitler and the

National Socialists, first becoming popular during World War I, which the Imperial German government used as a type of propaganda to rally all Germans—rich and poor, young and old—to the military cause. The Nazis used the concept to set their enemies apart from the larger German population. For instance, they argued that the communists only wanted to turn Germans against each other based on class differences, while Jews were not a true part of the "volk."

## When Was *Mein Kampf* Written?

Adolf Hitler's autobiography and political testament, *Mein Kampf* (*My Struggle*), was written in 1925 while he was serving time in prison for his role in the failed Munich Beer Hall putsch and was published by the National Socialist Party in two volumes in 1925 and 1926. In the book, Hitler goes into detail about why he believed Germany lost World War I, his reasons for being anti-Semitic, his hatred of communism, and his belief that Germanic peoples are racially superior to all others. After it was first published, *Mein Kampf* quickly became a worldwide best seller—partly due to the global prevalence of anti-Semitism, but also because people were curious to learn more about Hitler—and was published in most European languages as well as Hindi, Japanese, and Arabic.

## How Did Adolf Hitler and the National Socialists Come to Power?

Hitler and the National Socialist German Workers' Party came to power legally in the 1932 elections. The German government held two elections for the Reichstag—the German equivalent of Congress or the House of Commons—and one for president. The Reichstag elections were the most important because they would determine which party controlled the government. Elections were held on July 31, 1932 after the coalition running the government collapsed. Hitler and the

Nazi Party shocked everyone, but themselves, by winning 37% of the vote, nearly fourteen million votes, and taking 230 seats in the Reichstag to become the largest single party, although without a majority. A presidential election was held in March and then another federal Reichstag election was conducted on November 6, 1932 because the Nazis failed to form a governing coalition after the previous election. The result was a slight downturn in performance, as they only took 33% of the vote, but 196 seats, which kept them in their position as the largest party. Believing that the situation could be alleviated by acquiescing to some of Hitler's demands, President Hindenburg offered the office of Chancellor to Hitler, which he accepted on January 30, 1933.

## Who Was Ernst Thälmann?

Ernst Thälmann (1886-1944) was the leader of the German Communist Party (KPD) during the Weimar Republic and a major contender for the presidency in the 1932 German Presidential Election. Thälmann was introduced to Marxist ideology as a young dock worker in Hamburg, before being drafted to fight in World War I. After deserting on the Western Front, Thälmann returned to Germany where he did not face prosecution due to the change in government. He entered politics and rose quickly in the Communist Party, becoming the party's presidential candidate in 1925 and 1932. In the 1932 election he ran against incumbent Paul von Hindenburg and a host of other candidates, including the National Socialist German Workers' Party's Adolf Hitler. Thälmann made it into a runoff between him, Hindenburg, and Hitler, but only captured just over 10% of the vote compared to Hitler's 37% and Hindenburg's 53%. After the Nazis came to power, Thälmann was arrested on March 3, 1933 and held in solitary confinement until he was executed on August 18, 1944.

## Was the Reichstag Fire a Conspiracy?

When the Reichstag, the German congressional building in Berlin, burned on February 27, 1933, arson was quickly determined to be the cause. A Dutch communist named Marinus van der Lubbe was arrested and later executed for the crime, but many in the Nazi Party believed that it was part of a wider communist plot while others thought that it was a Nazi false flag operation. Those who believe that the arson was a false flag operation point out that almost immediately after the fire, Hitler pressured President von Hindenburg into ordering an emergency decree that suspended civil liberties, essentially giving the Nazi Party unlimited power. Although van der Lubbe insisted he acted alone, four other men— Ernst Togler, Georgi Dimitrov, Blagoi Popov, and Vasil Tanev, who were all members of different communist organizations—were tried with him for the arson. Lubber was sentenced to death but the other three men were acquitted and deported to the Soviet Union. Although there is consensus among modern historians that van der Lubbe played a role in the arson, there continue to be wide ranging theories as to whether he had help or if the Nazis in fact set him up for the task in order to take advantage of the situation.

## When Did Hindenburg Die?

Paul von Hindenburg, President of the Weimar Republic, died on August 2, 1934. Hindenburg was born on October 2, 1847 to a noble Prussian family and like most Prussians of his class he went on to become an officer in the Prussian Army and after unification with the Imperial German Army. A veteran of the Austro-Prussian War (1866), the Franco-Prussian War (1870-1871), and World War I (1914-1918), Hindenburg was well respected across all classes and in all regions of Germany. He won the presidency in 1925, which he held until his death at the age of eighty-six from lung cancer. Although one could certainly call Hindenburg a militarist and a conservative, he was not a fascist and did not particularly like Hitler. Still, he liked the Communists and Socialists even less so he was willing to make Hitler the chancellor and later suspended civil liberties after the Reichstag fire, which essentially made the National Socialist Party the sole rulers of Germany.

## How Long Did it Take for the Versailles Treaty to Be Undone?

The total process for Germany to dismantle the Versailles Peace Treaty took just over three years. The Treaty of Versailles, which officially ended World War I, was signed by representatives of Germany on June 28, 1919. It immediately took 13% of Germany's territory, decimated the military, and imposed economically crippling reparations on the country. The terms of the Treaty were a major factor in the rise of Adolf Hitler and the National Socialist Party, so when the Nazis took power they immediately began dismantling it. From 1933 to 1936 the terms of the Versailles Treaty were abolished by Hitler one point at a time. First, Hitler told the victors of World War I in no uncertain terms that Germany was done making reparations payments. Next, Germany began rearming its military and finally, in 1935 a plebiscite was held in the Saar region where 90% voted for union with Germany. On March 7, 1936, German troops marched into the demilitarized Rhineland, which combined with the previous actions officially negated the Versailles Treaty.

## What Were the Nuremberg Laws?

The Nuremberg Laws were two laws passed by the Nazi Party on September 15, 1935 that banned marriage between Germans and those deemed "non-Aryan," particularly Jews, and denied citizenship to Jews, among other things. The Reich Citizenship Law of November 14, 1935 further defined in detail how much Jewish ancestry a person could have and still be considered a citizen. The law determined that a person with less than half Jewish ancestry could be a citizen. These laws were later used to identify Jews, who were required to wear a yellow Star of David emblem on their clothing in public.

## When Did *Kristallnacht* Happen?

*Kristallnacht*, the "Night of Broken Glass," took place on the evening of November 9, 1938 across Germany. Over the course of the evening and into the early morning hours of the next day, thousands of Jewish businesses and synagogues were vandalized and burned and individual Jews were assaulted. The attacks were coordinated by the SA leadership and carried out by storm troopers, but other members of the German populace also got involved. When the smoke cleared, 177 synagogues were completely destroyed and 7,500 Jewish businesses burned to the ground.

## When Was Leni Riefenstahl Born?

Leni Riefenstahl was born Helene Bertha Amalie Riefenstahl on August 22, 1902 in Berlin, German Empire. Helen, or "Lennie" as she became known as, exhibited artistic talents from an early age, which she used to make a living, bringing her into acquaintance with the upper echelon of the Nazi Party. Riefenstahl experimented with what was at the time the fairly new medium of film by making several propaganda pieces for the Nazis. By far, her most famous work was the film of the Nazi's 1934 rally in Nuremberg, which was titled *Triumph des Willens* (*Triumph of the Will*). After the war, Riefenstahl was deemed a Nazi sympathizer and subject to

De-Nazification, but not charged with any crimes against humanity or war crimes. Leni Riefenstahl died on September 8, 2003 at the age of 101.

## How Did the Third Reich Get Its Name?

The German word "reich" translates into English as "empire," so therefore the "Third Reich" refers to the third great German empire. Since the National Socialist Party was fascist, it invoked the glories of its national past, which included what it saw as the two greatest preceding empires: the Holy Roman Empire of the Middle Ages, which was dissolved in 1806, and unified Imperial Germany from 1871 until it was dissolved after World War I in 1918. Both the National Socialists and their enemies often referred to Nazi Germany as the Third Reich.

## What Role Did Volkswagen Have in World War II?

The Volkswagen car company, best known for the "Beetle" and "Bus" models of automobiles, was established in 1937 to build cars for all the German people, so the name, which is translated into English as "People's Car." It was originally a state company under the aegis of the state workers' union organization, German Labor Front, with its factory in the city of Wolfsburg. After the war began, Volkswagen switched to produce primarily military vehicles, using much of its labor from prisons and concentration camps.

## Was the Autobahn System Built for the German Military?

Contrary to what many think, the *Autobahn*, Germany's extensive freeway system, was not built for the military. Nazi-era military transport was conducted overwhelmingly by train and the scarcity of gasoline during World War II limited the extensive use of trucks. The idea that the Autobahn system was built for the military is probably derived from the American Interstate system, which was started in the 1950s as a transportation network that could potentially be used during wartime. With that said, Adolf Hitler was a proponent of the system and hundreds of thousands of men were employed before the war to work on the project. By the time World War II began, more than 2,000 miles of the Autobahn were completed.

## How Did the Concept of Lebensraum Contribute to World War II?

Lebensraum, which translates from German into English as "living space," was the idea that the German people needed more land for the Third Reich. The Nazis believed in a very racialist form of fascism where all of the world's races were divided into a hierarchy and even within Europe there was a pecking order. The Nazis believe that the Nordic Europeans were superior and that their numbers should be expanded through a combination of increased birth rates and conquest of eastern Europe. The Slavic peoples of eastern Europe were considered to be inferior, so their lands were targeted for conquest and they were to be driven away, killed, and/or enslaved.

## What Does *Anschluss* Mean?

Anschluss is a German word that roughly translate into English as "joining." In the context of World War II, Anschluss refers to the German annexation, or reunification according to the Nazis, of Austria in 1938. Since Austria was an overwhelmingly and traditionally an ethnic German country, and Hitler was himself of Austrian origin, most of Europe's leaders had little concern about Germany's actions or motives. On March 12, 1938, German troops entered Austria and on March 15 they

16

marched through Vienna to largely cheering crowds, thereby formally joining Austria to the Third Reich.

## What Is an Autarkic Country?

An autarkic country is one whose economy is entirely, or almost entirely self-contained. Therefore, an autarky is a country that can support itself with its own resources without having to rely on exports. Hitler's second-in-command, Herman Göring, was named Plenipotentiary of the Four Year Plan in 1936, which was intended to make Germany an autarky within that span. Along with the move to autarky, Germany rearmed its military in violation of the Versailles Treaty.

# IN THE UNITED KINGDOM

## Why did South Africa Fare Better than the Other British Colonies during the Great Depression?

In the early twentieth century, South Africa was in possession of some of the most valuable and largest gold and diamond mines in the world. Throughout world history gold has always held value and has continued to do so even in periods of extreme monetary deflation and inflation. Gold became so valuable that many nations, including the United States, confiscated gold from its citizens. Because of this, Britain relied heavily on South Africa during the 1930s for economic support.

## When Did the United Kingdom Establish the "Sterling Zone"?

The United Kingdom established the sterling zone in 1931 when it left the gold standard. By the end of World War I the gold standard started to unravel as nations were unable to pay for their war debts, with the final blow to the economic regime being the Great Depression. In order to alleviate the effects of the Depression and to integrate the dominion nations, which were gradually becoming independent, the British government made the pound the monetary standard among all member nations, which became known as the sterling zone or sterling bloc. The move helped stabilized Britain and its colonies' economy during the Great Depression and prepared them for World War II.

## Did Canada Join the Sterling Zone?

No. Canada became an independent nation in 1931 but was still part of the British Commonwealth. Despite still being connected to Britain, Canada and Newfoundland, which did not join Canada until 1949, continued to use the dollar as their currency. Canada's close proximity to, and culture and economic connections with the United States was the primary reason for it staying on the dollar.

## Who Was Oswald Mosely?

Sir Oswald Ernald Mosely (1896-1980) was a British noble and politician who was notable for his support of the fascist regimes in Germany and Italy. He founded the British Union of Fascists (BUF) in 1932, whose platform resembled that of the Nazi Party in Germany. Besides its platform, the BUF adopted the typical style of a fascist organization of the era, with its own flag and a black clad security force. Despite the violence that often accompanied BUF rallies, Mosely enjoyed some popularity before the war and the membership of the BUF was steadily growing until Britain declared war on Germany. Mosely and his wife were imprisoned under "Defense Regulation 18B" for the entirety of the war without a trial, although in considerably better conditions than other non-noble fascists who were also interned under the same law.

## Why Did Chamberlin "Appease" Hitler?

Neville Chamberlin (1869-1940), the Prime Minister of the United Kingdom from May 1937 to May 1940, is often derided for "giving" the German speaking Sudetenland region to Nazi Germany in the September 19, 1938 Munich Agreement. The answer to the question, though, is somewhat complicated. Chamberlin believed that the French would be unwilling to support Britain at that point if it came to war and the United States was certainly out of the question. Therefore, allowing Germany to take the ethnic German region seemed like a reasonable alternative to war and allowed the British more time to prepare. He did not know that the Germans would annex all of Czechoslovakia in March 1939. Although Chamberlin's reputation is still mixed, it has garnered more sympathy in recent years.

# IN FRANCE

## What Was the Maginot Line?

The Maginot Line was a series of fortifications, bunkers, and walls that the French government installed along the French-German border during the 1930s. As the Germans rearmed after the National Socialists came to power in 1932, French Minister of War, André Maginot, came up with an ambitious plan to protect France through a series of fortifications along the two countries' shared border. The Maginot Line proved to be impenetrable, but the Germans forces instead invaded through the Low Countries in May 1940. Although the French and British high command anticipated the Germans flanking the Maginot Line through the Low Countries, they did not think they would attempt to traverse the dense Ardennes Forest. When the Germans went through the Ardennes, it marked the beginning of the fall of France.

## What Were the Locarno Treaties?

The Locarno Treaties were seven peace treaties signed in Locarno, Switzerland in October 1925 between the Allied powers of World War I, Germany's Weimar government, and some of the newly formed governments in central and eastern Europe. The Locarno Treaties essentially validated many of the main points of the Treaty of Versailles, which in France was believed to be sign of a new ear of European peace. The good feelings became known as the "spirit of Locarno" in France and some other western European nations; but those feelings quickly went to the wayside when the Great Depression hit and the Weimar government collapsed in Germany.

## What Was Action Française?

The tide of populism that brought fascist parties into power in Germany and Italy and nationalist governments in Spain, Romania, and Hungary was also active in France. Action Française formed in 1899 as a far right-wing political movement that favored a strong military and desired to bring the monarchy back to France. It was also strongly opposed to Marxism and communism and many of its members were not averse to fighting their political opponents in the streets. In the years before World War II the organization began to fracture, with moderates joining mainstream conservative parties and the more radical members forming openly fascist groups. Germany's occupation of France further fractured the group. Some members collaborated with the Vichy regime while others joined the French Resistance, sometimes even fighting alongside communists they once despised.

# IN ITALY

## Why Was Benito Mussolini Called "Il Duce"?

Benito Mussolini (1883-1945), the leader of Italy's National Fascist Party and primer minster of the country from 1922 to 1943, was known by his followers as *Il Duce*, which is Italian for "the leader." The sobriquet came from the fascist ideology, which was a belief in ultra-nationalism and the country being led by a strong leader, usually resulting in a type of cult of personality. Adolf Hitler was similarly known as *der Führer* in Germany, which also translates in English to "the leader,," although Mussolini earned his nickname much earlier than his German counterpart. Like many early twentieth century fascists, Mussolini flirted with far leftwing politics before becoming a fascist, while keeping some socialist economic ideas as part of his political platform.

## What Are the Origins of Fascism?

Unlike communism, which can trace its origins directly to nineteenth century philosopher Karl Marx. Some of the basic tenets of fascism were the following: ultra-nationalism and patriotism, an economic system that is neither fully socialist or capitalist, strong beliefs in the national past and traditions, extensive use of symbol, a specific style and lexicon, and a tendency to target certain groups as enemies of the people. Ancient Roman symbols were popular among both the German National Socialists and the Italian National Fascists: the stiff armed Nazi salute was actually a Roman era salute and the ancient Roman fasces, a bundle of sticks tied together with an axe, became the symbol of the Italian Fascists. But since fascism was nationalistic and there was no single fascist philosopher as the originator of the ideology, it varied from country to country. For instance, Italian fascism was far less anti-Semitic than in Germany.

**When Was the March on Rome?**

Beginning on October 28, 1922, Benito Mussolini, the leader of the National Fascist Party, led a march with 30,000 of his followers to Rome. At the vanguard of the Fascists were the members of the National Fascist Party's paramilitary branch, the "Black Shirts." The marchers arrived in Rome the next day and took power without firing a shot—Italy's king handed power to Mussolini legally and in a nonviolent manner.

# IN JAPAN

## What Role Did Militarism Play in World War II Japan?

After Japan modernized during the Meiji Period, it outlawed many of its feudal traditions, including the samurai class, in an effort to keep up with the industrialized, imperialistic Western countries. It accomplished its goal through the formation of a strong military and the modernization of its economy and industries. Its quick success was phenomenal, but despite outlawing some of the feudal traditions, their spirit remained. As Japan built its military through policies such as mandatory conscription, it incorporated many ultra-nationalist ideas at the political level and borrowed heavily from European fascism. Japanese militarism eventually led Japan into the Anti-Comintern Pact with Germany and Italy, making those three countries the primary Axis nations of World War II.

## What Was the Greater East Asia Co-Prosperity Sphere?

Much like its counterparts Italy and Germany, the Japanese military government before and during World War II desired to enforce its political, economic, and cultural will on its neighbors. The Japanese military government started using the somewhat benign sounding term "Greater East Asia Co-Prosperity Sphere" to project the image to the world that it was only looking after the interests of its smaller, militarily weaker Asian neighbors against the Western powers. During World War II the term became synonymous with Imperial Japan.

## How Did the Japanese "Rising Sun" Flag Originate?

The modern Japanese flag is a white banner with a red disk, which represents the sun. The sun is representative of Japan's nickname, "the land of the rising sun," but is also connected to the country's Shinto religious beliefs. According to Shintoism, the Japanese emperor is a descendant of the sun, so the sun plays a central role in many aspects of Japanese culture. The "Rising Sun Flag," which is a traditional Japanese flag with rays emanating from the sun, has come to be thought of as Japan's national flag during World War II, but it was actually the flag of the Imperial Navy. The Rising Sun Flag originated in seventeenth century feudal Japan and is still used today by the Japanese navy.

## Who Was Hideki Tojo?

Hideki Tojo was the Prime Minister of Japan from October 17, 1941 to July 22, 1944. Tojo came from a poor but respectable family: his father's side was from the former samurai class and his mother's father was a Buddhist priest. He was a workaholic and career military man who quickly rose through the ranks of Japan's militarist government in the early twentieth century. Tojo took part in the planning of and authorized the Japanese attack on Pearl Harbor. After the war, Tojo was tried by the International Military Tribunal for the Far East for war crimes, convicted, and sentenced to death. He executed by hanging on December 23, 1948.

## Who Was the Emperor of Japan during World War II?

On December 26, 1926, Hirohito became the 124th Emperor of Japan. Like the monarchs of Europe, Hirohito's power was limited; but by all accounts he supported the military's actions before and during World War II and was in favor of the alliance with Germany and Italy. The first time Hirohito was heard by his people was when he announced Japan's surrender on August 15, 1945, which due to the type of language he used, was only understood by the most educated Japanese. After the war, American prosecutors believed that Hirohito did not wield enough power to be held responsible for war crimes, so he was not prosecuted and was allowed to continue his reign as emperor. With that said, many scholars and experts believe that Hirohito was equally culpable of war crimes as some of Japan's leaders who were executed.

## What Was "State Shinto"?

Shintoism, the indigenous religion of Japan, stresses ancestor worship, belief in elemental deities, the importance of rituals, and a general respect for Japan's historical past. Since the Medieval Period, Shinto coexisted alongside other imported religions and philosophies such as Buddhism and Confucianism, but when Japan quickly modernized in the eighteenth century under the Meiji Constitution, the government began to meld Shintoism with government practices by promoting ideas such as emperor worship and the state control of shrines. By the time Japan invaded Manchuria, Shintoism was an integral part of the nationalist ideology of the state. The term was actually coined by the Americans after the war, who outlawed its use in favor of traditional, non-state sponsored Shintoism.

# IN THE WORLD

## What Is Eugenics?

Eugenics is the belief that selective breeding, and/or the restricting of breeding, including infanticide, within human populations can increase the overall quality of a society. Several ancient societies practiced various degrees of eugenics, but with the advent of modern medicine and scientific techniques it became a very popular idea in many Western nations in the late eighteenth and early twentieth centuries. Eugenics programs were popular in the early twentieth century in the United States, but it was in Nazi Germany where it was made into a state sponsored science. Those deemed to be of especially good racial stock were encouraged to have children and subsidized by the state to do so, while those deemed inferior were sometimes sterilized or euthanized.

## How Did Zionism Impact World War II?

As nationalist movements took hold of Europe during the nineteenth century, the spirit influenced European Jewry in the form of Zionism. Largely the result of Hungarian Jew Theodor Herzl's (1860-1904) writings and activism, Zionism is the belief that Palestine is the homeland of the world's Jewish population. European Jews began migrating to Palestine in large numbers in the late nineteenth century, which the Nazis began to view as a possible solution to their "Jewish problem" when they came to power. There was some collaboration between Zionist leaders and the Nazis before the war, but after the war began the Nazis changed their strategy to concentration camps and mass killings. Zionism then played an important role after the war as Jews displaced by the war fled to Palestine, which became the Jewish state of Israel, realizing Herzl's original dream.

## What Was the Polish Corridor?

The Polish Corridor referred to a slice of the region of Pomerania bordering the Baltic Sea that was part of Poland, but separated German East Prussia from the rest of Germany before World War II. Due to numerous wars and the rise and fall of several different kingdoms going back to the Middle Ages, Pomerania had a mixture of German and Polish people. The region was part of the German Empire before World War I, but per the Versailles Treaty it was given to Poland because the majority of the region was Polish and Poland desired access to the Baltic Sea. An exodus of Germans from the region to either contiguous Germany or East Prussia followed, leading to tension between the two countries. Taking back the Polish corridor was one of the planks of the Nazi Party platform.

## What Role Did the Great Depression Play in World War II?

In the United States, many Americans think of the Great Depression as an American only catastrophe, but it was a worldwide phenomenon that had wide-ranging effects, many of which contributed to World War II. A number of factors led to the Great Depression, but the straw that broke the camel's back was the stock market crash, often referred to as "Black Tuesday," of October 29, 1929. Over speculation caused the market to lose 40% of its value, causing many to withdraw money from banks, which in turn caused banks to close. The situation was compounded by a housing market collapse caused by a credit crunch and finally the Dust Bowl in the Great Plains proved to be the icing on top of the financial disaster cake. Although the world was far less integrated in the 1930s than it is today, there still was a global economy, so the situation in the United States spread to

Europe. By 1932, fourteen million Americans were unemployed, six million in Germany, and about three million were jobless in the United Kingdom. The Great Depression helped bring Adolf Hitler and the National Socialists to power in Germany in 1932 and Franklin Delano Roosevelt won the American presidential election that same year. Neither probably would have been elected if it were not for the global economic problems.

## What Were Some of the Impacts of the 1935 Italian Invasion of Ethiopia/Abyssinia?

On October 3, 1935, the Kingdom of Italy, whose government was controlled by Benito Mussolini and the National Fascist Party, invaded the east African nation of Abyssinia, now known as Ethiopia. It took the Italians over a year to completely occupy the country and at the expense of 10,000 men, but pockets of Ethiopian resistance continued until the end of World War II. The invasion garnered sympathy for Abyssinia and exposed the Italian military as being a rung below its major European rivals. Most importantly, the Italian invasion and occupation of Abyssinia demonstrated that the League of Nations was a reckless organization, as both Italy and Abyssinia were members, but it could do nothing substantial to punish Italy for the invasion.

## Why Did the League of Nations Fail to Maintain Peace in the 1930s?

Historians often point to the ineffectiveness of the League of Nations as one of the reasons for World War II. Mussolini's invasion of Abyssinia, the Spanish Civil War, the Winter War, the invasion of Manchuria, and the invasion and annexing of Poland were all events that took place before or at the beginning of World War II that if dealt with effectively on an international level, may have prevented worldwide war. The structure of the League failed to consider shifting alliances and the nature of the global economy, which meant that nations usually pursued their own best interest instead of the League's. Most importantly, unlike the United Nations today, the League of Nations had no enforcement wing in the form of an armed force it could send to trouble zones.

# CHAPTER 2:

# THE FIRST SHOTS ARE FIRED

## EARLY BATTLES AND TACTICS: PACIFIC THEATER

### Why Did Japan Invade Manchuria?

Japan invaded Manchuria on September 19, 1931, which essentially started World War II in the Pacific, almost eight years before Germany invaded Poland. As Japan's militarist and imperialist philosophies became institutionalized, it began expanding throughout Asia beginning in the early twentieth century. Manchuria, which was part of China at the time, bordered Japanese held Korea and so the Japanese military thought that it would be the next logical choice of territory for them to take. On September 18, members of the Japanese army conducted a false flag bombing on a railroad track that did little damage, but served as a pretext for the invasion. The Japanese army moved without the civilian government's approval, demonstrating that it was the generals and admirals who held all the power in Japan.

### What Was the Marco Polo Bridge Incident?

The Marco Polo Bridge Incident was a conflict between the Chinese and Japanese militaries from July 7 through July 9,

1937. After conquering Manchuria and installing a puppet government, Imperial Japan turned its eyes toward China proper. The Japanese military already had a presence in China from the nineteenth century and on the evening of July 7 were conducting maneuvers near the city of Wanping, which is about ten miles from the capital of Peking/Beijing when one of their soldiers went missing. After being refused entry into Wanping, the Japanese military attacked the walled city but were repulsed. Chinese reinforcements arrived to successfully stop the Japanese forces from crossing the bridge, but the incident provided the Japanese with the *causes belli* they needed for a full-scale war against China. The Marco Polo Bridge Incident proved to be the first shots in the Second Sino-Japanese War, which was essentially a sub-theater of the Pacific Theater of World War II.

## What Was the Rape of Nanking?

The "Rape of Naking," also known as the "Nanjing Massacre," took place in Nanjing/Nanking, China between December 1937 and January 1938 just after the Japanese Army took control of the city. During the six week period after the Japanese first occupied the city, they committed numerous atrocities against the Chinese citizens, including murder, rape, robbery, and vandalism. It is estimated that between 50,000 and 300,000 civilians were killed during the massacre. Many of the victims were shot, but several were hacked to death with samurai swords, which were actually documented by the Japanese in photographs. After the war, some of the Japanese officers involved with the massacre were convicted and executed for war crimes.

## What Role Did the Mitsubishi Corporation Play in the Japanese War Effort?

Today, Mitsubishi is best known for making cars, but during World War II it manufactured Japan's best fighter plane—the

A6M Zero. The Zero as it was commonly known as, or often "Zeke" pejoratively by the Allies. It was first went into service in 1939 and remained the primary long-distance, carrier fighter used by the Imperial Japanese Navy until the end of the war. The Zero dominated the skies over the Pacific in the early stages of the war and was instrumental in the attack on Pearl Harbor.

### When Did the Office of Civilian Defense Form?

The United States federal agency, the Office of Civilian Defense (OCD) was formed on May 21, 1941 by an executive order from President Roosevelt. As the Axis powers steadily expanded their territories, Americans began to fear that their country was the next target. In order to better prepare the country in case an invasion or attack were to happen, Roosevelt and others in the government believed it was imperative to modernize America's civil defense network. The president reactivated the Council of National Defense and formed the OCD to serve the public in case of attack. The Civil Air Patrol (CAP), which was a civilian auxiliary of the Army Air Force, was then created on December 1, 1941, just days before the Pearl Harbor attack.

### What Were the Circumstances of the Invasion of French Indochina?

The French colony of Indochina, which is today the nation-states of Vietnam, Cambodia, and Laos, found itself in a strange position once World War II officially began. When Germany invaded France and imposed an armistice in June 1940, the northern half of the country was German occupied while the southern half and its colonies were under control of the "Vichy Government." That same month Japanese officials demanded of their French counterparts in Indochina that all routes to China be closed, as they were conducting military operations. Although the French complied, the Japanese invaded northern Indochina on September 22 in order to assume complete control of the region. The French offered only limited resistance, with many units surrendering; fighting was done by September 26 and the Japanese were in control of the northern part of the colony. On July 28, 1941, the Japanese invaded southern Indochina in order to prepare for their operations in the south Pacific, but they allowed the Vichy French officials to stay in power until 1944.

# EARLY BATTLES AND TACTICS: EUROPEAN THEATER

## What Role Did the Spanish Civil War Play in World War II?

From 1936 through 1939 Spain was gripped by civil war between factions of the far-right and far-left of the political spectrum. Knowing that the war could perhaps be a "dress rehearsal" for things to come and also wanting to promote their own interests, the Soviet Union, Germany, and Italy supported and funded factions sympathetic to their ideologies, thereby making it a proxy war. Germany was particularly active in its support of the Nationalists, sending airpower and a volunteer unit to Spain known as the "Condor Legion." The Nationalists under General Francisco Franco won the war and later repaid Germany and Italy by remaining neutral in World War II, but allowing Spanish volunteers to fight the Soviet Union on the Eastern Front. After World War II, Franco also gave many accused Nazi war criminals sanctuary in Spain.

## What Was the Wehrmacht?

Although the German Army was often referred to as the Wehrmacht, it was actually the name for the entire German armed forces during the Nazi regime and included the Army (*Heer*), Navy (*Kriegsmarine*), and Airforce (*Luftwaffe*). Wehrmacht is literally translated into English as "Defense Force" or "Defense Power." The Wehrmacht's early success on the battlefield was due to a combination of able officers, a dedicated corps of enlisted men, and the willingness to employ new tactics. Besides blitzkrieg, the Wehrmacht developed camouflage uniforms and was the first military to use paratroopers extensively. The Wehrmacht was also unique from the other militaries during World War II in that its air force was a specific branch of the military and primarily land based. The Waffen SS, which was the military arm of the SS, was a separate military and unconnected to the Wehrmacht, although commanders from both forces worked together during campaigns.

## Why Did Stalin Sign the Molotov-Ribbentrop Pact?

The Molotov-Ribbentrop Pact, often referred to as the Nazi-Soviet Pact, was a neutrality/non-aggression agreement signed between Nazi Germany and the Soviet Union on August 23, 1939 in Moscow. Named for the Soviet and Germany foreign ministers, Vyacheslav Molotov and Joachim von Ribbentrop respectively, such an agreement seemed impossible at the time due to the ideological differences between the two countries. It is believed that Stalin thought the Western nations would abandon the Soviet Union to Germany anyway, so he went ahead with the agreement to possibly forestall the inevitable. A secret proviso in the agreement essentially gave the Baltic countries to Stalin, which allowed him to expand the growing Soviet Empire.

## What Are the Origins of the Word "Panzer"?

Panzer is a German word that means "armor," but before and during World War II it was used more specifically to refer to tanks. Tank warfare was introduced in World War I, but surprisingly the Germans built very few tanks in that war. Between the wars, the German high command began to see the utility of using tanks in organized divisions, or *panzerdivision*. Early German tanks were not much better than their French or British counterparts and often had weaker armor, but were utilized much better in formations by their commanders. The later Panther and Tiger tanks proved to be more formidable in terms of armor and firepower. The term "panzer" is still used by the German military and even sometimes used in other languages to refer to modern tanks.

## What Role Did Blitzkrieg Play in World War II?

Blitzkrieg, translated into English as "lightning war," was first termed by Western journalists to describe the incredibly fast and effective German assault on Poland. It was a new type of warfare that relied on fast moving tanks and mechanized infantry backed up by fighter and bomber planes. Blitzkrieg played an enormous role in the first few campaigns of the war, giving the Germans a tremendous advantage, but much less so once the Allies went on the offensive. Blitzkrieg was also not much of a major factor in North Africa.

## When Did the First Naval Battle of World War II Happen?

The first naval battle of World War II took place on December 13, 1939 in the Rio de la Plata estuary off the coast of Uruguay. The German pocket battleship/cruiser, *Admiral Graf Spee*, was commissioned by the German Kriegsmarine in 1936 and was one of the first ships of its class to see battle in the Atlantic. After the war began and it was clear that the British would not come to a peace treaty with Germany, the *Admiral Graf Spee* was ordered to attack British shipping vessels in the Atlantic Ocean. In September 1939, the *Admiral Graf Spee* began attacking British merchant vessels in the south Atlantic, which made it a prime target for the British navy. On December 13, two British light cruisers and a heavy cruiser— the *HMS Achilles 4*, the *HMS Ajax 7*, and the *HMS Exeter 61* respectively— caught up to the *Admiral Graf Spee*. Although the German vessel had the combined British squadron outgunned, there was a British blockade in the north Atlantic, which gave the British more flexibility. Admiral Hans Langsdoff of the *Admiral Graf Spee* attacked the British squadron, but after a more than two hour battle he ordered a retreat to the harbor of Montevideo. Prevented from leaving the harbor by Uruguayan officials, Langsdorf scuttled the ship in the harbor and committed suicide on December 19.

## What Was the Winter War?

From November 30, 1939 to March 13, 1940, Finland fought a war of survival against the Soviet Union's mighty Red Army in what became known as the Winter War. While the world's eyes were on Germany just after it had invaded Poland, Joseph Stalin sent the Red Army to invade Finland over perceived diplomatic slights and the desire to take the Aaland Archipelago and the city of Vipurri/Viborg. Led by Field Marshal Carl Gustav Mannerheim, the Fins used the terrain to their advantage and non-conventional military methods to slow the Soviet assault. Although the Soviets took Viborg and technically won the war, the Finns survived to join Germany in its war against the Soviet Union on the Eastern Front.

## What Was the "Phoney War"?

After Germany invaded Poland on September 1, 1939, France and the United Kingdom declared war on Germany two days later, but did not attack. For the next seven months there was no fighting in the west, although most people knew it was inevitable, so the British began referring to the period as the "Phoney War." American newspapers picked up the term and used the traditional British spelling instead of the American. The Phoney War ended when Germany invaded Denmark and Norway on April 9, 1940.

## How Effective Were the British Matilda Tanks?

After Britain declared war on Germany in 1939, it sent the British Expeditionary Force (BEF) to France, which was primarily infantry, but there were enough tanks to comprise the 1st Army Tank Brigade. The Tank Brigade was comprised of fifty-eight Matilda I (A11) and sixteen Matilda II (A12) tanks. The Matilda I was a small, two crew tank with a single gun, while the Matilda II was slightly larger with a three man crew and a more powerful gun. Both Matilda models were better armored than the German panzers and did quite well against their adversaries. Matildas were used in the counter-offensive against Rommel and his panzer at Arras on May 10, 1940 and despite requiting themselves well in that battle, were overcome by the German numbers and most of the battalion was lost. The remaining Matildas gave cover for the evacuation at Dunkirk. Although the Matilda I was shelved after 1940, the Matilda II was effectively used for the remainder of the war, especially in North Africa.

## What Was the Katyn Massacre?

When the Soviets annexed eastern Poland in September 1939, the Polish military was under orders not to engage the Red

Army, which made the occupation that much easier, as well as what came next. The NKVD, the Soviet secret police at the time, began rounding up all the high ranking Polish army and police officers, as well as influential intellectuals, and placed them in prison camps within western Russia. Once at the camps, the NKVD interrogated all of the prisoners in order to ascertain who were the leaders and the most influential among them and once that was determined those men were marked for execution. Between April and May 1940, up to 22,000 Polish and men of other ethnicities who served in the Polish army, were brought to the Katyn Forest near Smolensk, Russia and executed. Most of the victims were shot to death in large groups and buried in mass graves in the forest.

## What Was the Junker Ju 87 usually Known as?

The Junker Ju 87 dive bomber was known by the Germans and the Allies as the "Stuka" dive bomber. The Stuka was very recognizable due to its gull wings, but the plane was most known for making dives of several hundred feet, with an eerie siren blaring, to destroy enemy tanks. Stukas played a major role early in the war and were very effective against enemy tanks and heavily fortified infantry positions, but were very vulnerable to enemy fighters.

## Why Did Germany Invade Denmark and Norway?

The German invasion of Denmark and Norway, codenamed Operation Weserübung, began on April 9, 1940 and was completed on June 10, 1940. Initially, the Germans had no plans to invade Scandinavia, although Hitler wanted to eventually incorporate the Nordic peoples into his Greater German Reich. The invasion came about, though, when the French and British began planning their own invasion of

Norway, which they called "Plan R 4." The reason for the planned British-Franco invasion was to control the Baltic Sea shipping lanes in order to deprive Germany of iron ore that it was receiving from neutral Sweden. Tough terrain and amphibious landings made the operation difficult for the Germans, but they won an overwhelming victory, giving them momentum as they invaded the Low Countries.

## What Was Case Yellow?

Case Yellow, *Fall Gelb* in German, was the German plan for the invasion of the Low Countries of the Netherlands, Belgium, and Luxembourg, which was in preparation for the invasion of France. Case Yellow was first proposed by Hitler in his sixth directive on October 9, 1939. The German high-command considered different plans until the invasion of the Low Countries began in the early morning hours of May 10, 1940. Luxembourg fell in one day, the Netherlands in a week, and all resistance in Belgium was extinguished by the end of May.

## How Many Allied Casualties Were there in the Battle of Luxembourg?

Luxembourg, a tiny country tucked between Germany, France, and Belgium was invaded by Germany on May 10, 1940 as part of its Low Countries campaign, "Case Yellow." The Germans invaded in the early morning hours with over 50,000 men and were only met with light resistance from Luxembourg gendarmes. Although there were at least 18,000 French troops in the country, they all retreated behind the Maginot Line to await a German attack. Only five French troops died and one British pilot who was shot down and succumbed later to his injuries. No Luxembourgers were killed.

## How Long Did It Take France to Fall?

It took six weeks for France to collapse. The invasion of France was part of Case Yellow, although the Germans had to subdue the Low Countries first. The French had 117 divisions and the British thirteen divisions from the 2nd British Expeditionary Force (BEF) versus 141 German divisions. The French had more tanks but the Germans owned the skies. Beginning on May 12, the Germans faced a choke point at the Ardennes Forest around the French city of Sedan. Heavy fighting ensued but by the May 15 the French and British forces had retreated and the Germans had created a salient that stretched past the Ardennes. With the French Army all but destroyed and the BEF in retreat, French Prime Minister Paul Reynaud resigned and was replaced by Field Marshal Philippe Pétain, who surrendered France on June 22 in the Forest of Compiègne to Adolf Hitler. It was the same location where the Germans surrendered to the Allies to end World War I, so to add insult to injury Hitler had the railway car where from the World War I signing taken from a museum and brought to the forest for the French capitulation.

## What Was Operation Dynamo?

Operation Dynamo was the codename for the Allied evacuation of Dunkirk, France from May 26 through June 4, 1940. As the Germany Army surged through the Ardennes Forest during the Battle of France, thousands of Belgian, French, and British troops were cut off from the rest of the country and had to build defensive fortifications around the cities of Dunkirk and Lille as they waited for ships to evacuate them to England. For reasons that remain a mystery, the German halted their advance on May 24, which gave the British enough time to assemble a flotilla of naval and private ships consisting of everything from frigates to fishing boats.

More than 300,000 Allied soldiers were evacuated to Britain, many of whom fought later in North Africa and Europe.

## When Was the Afrika Korps Formed?

The Afrika Korps, which was the German expeditionary force in North Africa, was formed on January 11, 1941. Although Erwin Rommel was not the Afrika Korps' original commander, he led the force for most of its existence. The Afrika Korps was originally formed to support the Italians in Libya, who were having difficulties with the British Expeditionary Force, especially the British 7th Armoured Division (the Desert Rats). Under Rommel, the Afrika Korps had many early successes against the British, but were turned back from Egypt at the Second Battle of El-Alamein in November 1942. The Afrika Korps surrendered to the Americans on May 13, 1943.

## How Did Operation Barbarossa Get Its Name?

The German invasion of the Soviet Union on June 22, 1941, codenamed *Unternehmen Barbarossa* (Operation Barbarossa), was a surprise attack along a 1,800 mile front in eastern Europe. It involved close to four million military personal from nearly every Axis country—including: Germany, Hungary, Romania, Italy, Finland, Croatia, and volunteers from Spain— making it the largest military operation in history. Always attempting to resurrect the past in their favor, the Germans took the codename from Frederick I (1122-1190), who was the Holy Roman Emperor from 1155 until his death. Barbarossa is Italian for "red beard", which referred to his signature look, but Frederick I was known more as a tough fighter, conqueror, and crusader.

# IMPORTANT INDIVIDUALS AND GROUPS

## When Was Erwin Rommel Born?

Rommel was born Johannes Erwin Eugen Rommel on November 15, 1891 in Heidenheim, Empire of Germany. He was a World War I veteran, who through his intelligence and charisma was able to rapidly advance through the ranks of the Germany Army. His greatest success was in the early years of the war, which earned him the coveted title of Field Marshal in 1942. After being implicated in the July 20 Plot to assassinate Adolf Hitler in 1944, Rommel was arrested, but instead of trying him publicly, which would have made the regime look weak, Hitler "offered" Rommel the "choice" to commit suicide. Rommel died of a self-inflicted gunshot wound on October 14, 1944.

## When Was Heinz Guderian Born?

Heinz Guderian born on June 17, 1888 in Kulm/Chelmno, German Empire. A veteran of World War I, Guderian was impressed with the potential of mechanized and tank warfare and promoted the idea whenever he had the chance as he moved up through the ranks of the beleaguered German Army in the interwar years. Guderian played a key role in Germany's early success during the war, leading the victories in Poland, the Low Countries, and Barbarossa. When the war on the Eastern Front came to a halt, his role in the military diminished. After the war, Guderian helped establish West Germany's army. Guderian died on May 14, 1954 at the age of sixty-five in Schwangau, West Germany.

## How Did the Name "Quisling" Come to Mean "Traitor"?

Vidkum Abraham Lauritz Jonssøn Quisling (1887-1945) was a Norwegian diplomat and stateman who collaborated with the Nazis after Germany conquered Norway in April 1940. Quisling worked as a diplomat and spy throughout the early twentieth century, but by the 1930s he became intrigued with fascism and started the Nasjonal Samling Party (National Union). The Nazis were at first reluctant to work with Quisling, but made him Prime Minister of Norway in 1942. He cooperated with the Nazis by interning Norway's small Jewish community and by pursuing other pro-Nazi policies. After the war, Quisling was arrested by the new Norwegian government and charged with treason among other charges. He was convicted of the most serious charges and executed by a firing squad on October 24, 1945.

## When Was Isoroku Yamamoto Born?

Isoroku Yamamoto was born on April 4, 1884 in Nagaoka, Empire of Japan. He was adopted into a wealthy samurai family and pursued a career in the Imperial Navy, where he rose steadily in the ranks. Although somewhat of a maverick who was not afraid to oppose Japan's politicians, he was promoted to admiral in 1940 due to his success and forward thinking military ideas. In particular, Yamamoto promoted the concept of naval aviation, which proved to give Japan the edge early in the war. Yamamoto was killed on April 18, 1943 when American codebreakers learned that he was making a tour of Japanese bases in the South Pacific via airplane. When Yamamoto's course was learned, the order was given by President Roosevelt himself to shoot the admiral down.

## How Did the Axis Powers Get Its Name?

On November 1, 1936, after Germany and Italy officially signed a treaty the previous month, Benito Mussolini declared that the Rome-Berlin "axis" would control Europe. The members of the Axis powers grew from that point on, although the members never referred to their alliance as the "Axis," but instead by a number of other names. The first major alliance of fascist nations was the Anti-Comintern Pact (Anti-Communist International Pact), which was first signed by Germany and Japan in November 1936 and then Italy in 1937. The pact then officially became a military alliance known as the Tripartite Pact in 1940. Romania, Hungary, Bulgaria, Slovakia, and Croatia would all join the Tripartite Pact at later dates, although most also turned on the alliance late in the war. The Tripartite Pact became synonymous with "Axis" and sometimes included Finland and Thailand.

## When Did Churchill Deliver the "We Shall Fight on the Beaches" Speech?

British Prime Minister Winston Churchill gave perhaps his most famous and important speech, often known as the "We Shall Fight on the Beaches" speech, on June 4, 1940 to the House of Commons in London. Churchill delivered the speech after Germany had conquered the Low Countries, had just defeated France, and as thousands of British, French, and Belgian soldiers were being ferried across the English Channel in the Dunkirk evacuation. Despite Britain being in such a difficult position, the speech helped raise the morale of Britain's government and people.

## What Was the Iron Guard?

The Iron Guard was a Romanian fascist organization that was formed in 1927 by Corneliu Zelea Codreanu. Much like the

Fascists in Italy and the Nazis in Germany, the Iron Guard was anti-communist and high nationalistic. It was much more pro-Christian than the other fascist movements and based much of its anti-Jewish ideas more on religion than race, in contrast to the Nazi's racially based anti-Semitic ideas. Codreanu was imprisoned for his political activities and died escaping in 1938, which only made the movement more popular with rural and middle class Romanians. The Iron Guard formed an alliance with the existing Romanian government in September 1940. Although the Iron Guard was outlawed after it attempted to take complete power of the Romanian government in January 1941, its influence continued because in June 1941 Romania officially joined the Axis powers.

## When Was Rudolph Hess Born?

Rudolf Walter Richard Hess was born on April 26, 1894 in Alexandria, Egypt to a German merchant family. After spending the first few years of his life in Egypt, he was sent to Germany for his education and later embarked on a career in the military and politics. Hess was an early member of the National Socialist Party, served time in prison for his role in the Beer Hall Putsch, and later became Hitler's most trusted comrade. Once the Nazis came to power, Hess was made Deputy Führer, which made him the number two man in the government. On May 10, 1941 Hess flew a plane solo to Scotland to meet Douglas Douglas-Hamilton, whom he believed led the opposition in Britain to the war. Hess hoped that a deal could be arranged through back channels that would keep Britain out of the war before the start of Operation Barbarossa. After a harrowing flight that ended in Hess parachuting, he was captured by the British who were not interested in his peace overtures. Hitler publicly disavowed Hess to keep favor with the Italians and Japanese, making him for a time one of the most hated people in the war. He was later convicted of war crimes, sentenced to life imprisonment, and committed suicide in 1987 at the age of ninety-three.

## What Was Carl Gustav Emile Mannerheim's Nationality?

Despite his very German sounding name, Carl Mannerheim (1867-1951) was a Finnish national. Mannerheim was descended from Germans who immigrated to Swedish controlled Finland and married into the Swedish speaking elites. He is best known as the commander-in-chief of Finland's military against the Soviet Union during World War II, but he also served as Finland's Prime Minister after the war. Finland was actually part of Imperial Russia when Mannerheim was born, so his birth nationality was Russian and he served for many years in the Imperial Russian Army before Finland gained its independence in 1918.

## What Was Francisco Franco's Attitude Toward the Axis Powers?

General Francisco Franco (1892-1975), dictator of Spain from 1939 until his death, walked a fine line during World War II between the Axis and Allies. Although Italian and German military support helped him win the Spanish Civil War and come to power, he officially kept Spain neutral during the war. After Germany conquered France, Franco met Hitler on October 23, 1940 to discuss the idea of Spain joining the Axis powers. Hoping to take advantage of his country's position in western Europe and on the Mediterranean Sea, Franco requested Gibraltar and North Africa for Spain's participation, which Hitler refused. Despite not officially joining the Axis, Franco allowed Spanish volunteers to serve on the Eastern Front, allowed German and Italian ships to use Spanish ports, and also is said to have given the Nazis a list of Spanish-Jews. On the other hand, Franco forbade Spanish citizens from fighting the Allies on the Western Front and gave thousands of Jews asylum who were escaping German occupied Europe.

# CHAPTER 3:

# AXIS DOMINATION

## EVENTS, GROUPS, AND PEOPLE IN ASIA

### How Many Ships Did the Americans Lose at Pearl Harbor?

When the Japanese attacked Pearl Harbor, Hawaii on December 7, 1941, they had hoped to destroy the entire American Pacific fleet. It was actually a sound strategy because most of the fleet was harbored at the naval air station and navy yard in Pearl Harbor at the time. The Japanese attack also included bombing U.S. navy bases and airstrips throughout the island, but the attack on Pearl Harbor was to be the *coup de grace* that would knock the Americans out of the war in the Pacific before it even began. A total of twenty-one American ships in the harbor were severely damaged, but only three were destroyed. The most famous of the American ships destroyed was the *Arizona*, but the other ships destroyed were the *Oklahoma* and *Utah*. Many American destroyers were untouched and the submarine pens incurred very little damage

### How Did the Philippines Fall?

In 1898, as a result of the Spanish-American War, the Philippines became an American territory. In the early twentieth century, the Philippines became an important center for American interests in Asia as it had a number of military bases and was in the middle of Asian shipping lanes. On December 8, 1941, just hours after the attack on Pearl Harbor, Japan invaded the Philippines. The American naval fleet in the region was forced to retreat, which is when American General Douglas MacArthur famously uttered the words, "I shall return." American resistance continued until the spring, but without air and sea support it was squashed. Japanese control of the Philippines represented another piece in their growing Asian empire and a key strategic position from which to attack American and British positions in the Pacific.

## When Did the Battle of Hong Kong Begin?

Although the date that the Battle of Hong Kong began on was December 8, 1941, due to the International Date Line it took place at the same time as the Pearl Harbor attacks. The Japanese attacked the British colony of Hong Kong with nearly 30,000 troops, fifty planes, and several ships. The British garrison in Hong Kong was about half the Japanese force and comprised of a mix of British, Indian, Canadian, Chinese, and Free French troops. The Allies put up a stiff resistance until Christmas, when the Governor of Hong Kong, Mark Aitchison Young formerly surrendered to the Japanese.

## What Was the Bataan Death March?

After General George MacArthur left the Philippines Islands with most of the American forces, some were left behind to fight alongside the Filipinos against the Japanese. Most of the resistance took place around the Manila Bay with the Battle of Bataan beginning on January 7, 1942 and lasting until the Americans surrendered on April 9. The Japanese then had to move over 60,000 prisoners of war and more than 300,000 displaced civilians, which they were not prepared to do. The next day, American and Filipino prisoners were forcibly marched from Mariveles and Bagac in the Bataan province to the city of San Fernando where they were loaded onto trains and sent to a camp in the city of Capas, for a total journey of nearly seventy miles. Prisoners were beaten, robbed, and starved during the journey and many died of dehydration on the train ride. Up to 600 Americans died during the march, but the Filipinos fared much worse – some estimates are that up to 20,000 died during the Bataan Death March. After the war, Japanese General Masaharu Homma was convicted of war crimes for his role in the Bataan Death March and executed.

## How Was Japan Able to Conquer Southeast Asia so Quickly?

After taking the Philippines, Burma, the Dutch East Indies, Malaya, and Hong Kong, the Japanese next turned their eyes to the important city of Singapore, which was the last important base the British held in southeast Asia. After a week of heavy fighting, the Japanese occupied Singapore on February 15, 1942, all but completing their conquest of southeast Asia. The Japanese were able to take so much land so quickly by realizing that their fight was much different than the one in Europe. They relied more on infantry and when they did use tanks they were usually light tanks. The Japanese also often used bicycles to move their infantry in heavily forested and jungle areas.

## Besides the Philippines, Did the Japanese Occupy Any Other American Territory?

Yes, on June 3, 1942 a small Japanese force occupied the islands of Attu and Kiska on the far western edge of the Aleutian Islands archipelago of Alaska, which was at the time an American territory. The Japanese viewed Alaska as a possible American staging point for an invasion of Japan so they sent a force to occupy the sparsely populated islands of Attu and Kiska in preparation for a later, larger occupation. The Japanese force occupied the islands for over a year until they were driven out of Attu in May 1943. When a combined American-Canadian force arrived in Kiska Island in August 1943, they found it abandoned.

## When Was the Bombing of Darwin?

In an effort to prevent the Allies from using the Darwin harbor in Darwin, Australia to launch air and sea attacks into their empire, the Japanese bombed the city on February 19, 1942. On the day of the attack, there were sixty-five Allied ships in the harbor, which was only lightly guarded by sixteen anti-aircraft guns. The attack consisted of two separate air raids carried out by Japanese fighters and bombers that left from four aircraft carries, all of which participated in the attack on Pearl Harbor less than two months prior. The surprise attack left 236 Allied military personnel and civilians dead and hundreds wounded. Most importantly for the Japanese, they were able to destroy thirty Allied aircraft and sink eleven Allied ships.

## Why Did Thailand Align with Japan?

Thailand's position in World War II was quite complicated and somewhat similar to what happened to France. Before World War II, Thailand was a constitutional monarchy, but its Prime Minister, Phibun, assumed many dictatorial powers in 1938 including changing the name of the country from Siam to the more ethnically pronounced Thailand. Although officially neutral at the start of the war, Thailand had claims on French Indochina, which the Japanese used to their advantage. The Japanese wanted Thailand to allow them to use their land for bases to attack other countries in Asia, especially the British held colonies of Burma, Malaya and India, so they gave the Thais an ultimatum to either join them or be invaded. The Thai government initially resisted the Japanese threats, which led to an invasion on December 8, 1941. Seeing an opportunity to gain land in Indochina and feeling sympathy toward the Japanese cause, not to mention he had few options with Japanese troops occupying part of his country, Phibun signed an alliance with the Japanese. After numerous British and American bombing raids on Bangkok, Thailand officially declared war on the United Kingdom and the United States on January 25, 1942. While the Thai government officially sided with Japan, there were significant numbers of Thais, known as the Free Thai Movement, who forcefully resisted the Japanese throughout the war and formed their own government. Because Thailand essentially had two governments during the war and was in an impossible position, much as France was, the United States did not view Thailand as a true enemy power.

## When Did the Americans Begin Interning People of Japanese Descent?

The United States government began interning Japanese-Americans and people of Japanese descent on February 19, 1942. After the Japanese attack on Pearl Harbor, Americans began to look at Japanese immigrants and even Japanese-Americans with distrust, thinking that they may be spying for Japan or preparing to do acts of sabotage. This attitude was particularly prevalent along the West Coast, which is where many Americans believed would be the target of Japan's next attack. High ranking members of the military also believed that Japanese on the West Coast were potential spies, which led President Roosevelt to issue Executive Order 9066, the order to intern the Japanese. The entire West Coast was deemed an "exclusion area" to anyone of Japanese ancestry, so those living there were sent to "assembly centers" on the coast and then moved to internment camps in the interior. Up to 120,000 people of Japanese descent were interned during World War II, a majority of them American citizens. Most of those interned lost their homes, businesses, and livelihoods and had little to return home to. In 1988, President Ronald Reagan signed into law the Civil Liberties Act of 1988, which gave all survivors of the internment camps $20,000 and admitted that the U.S. Government was wrong in its treatment of Japanese-Americans and people of Japanese descent during World War.

## What Role Did Mahatma Gandhi Play in World War II?

Mahatma Gandhi (1869-1948) is best known as being the leader of India's independence movement, but he also played a not so minor role in World War II. Although Gandhi did not support Nazi Germany, Fascist Italy, or Imperial Japan, he opposed Indian involvement in the war based on the fact that India was still a colony of Britain. Gandhi urged his fellow Indians not to participate in the war effort and delivered many speeches on the subject, urging the British to "Quit India." Due to his anti-war efforts, the British authorities arrested Gandhi twice, holding him the second time for two years, not releasing him until near the end of the war in May 1944. The British released the seventy-five-year-old Gandhi due to ailing health, but he was more determined than ever to resist British rule over India.

## What Role Did Mao Zedong Play in World War II?

Mao Zedong (1893-1976) is best known as being the first leader of Communist China from 1949 until his death, but before that he played an important role in World War II as a resistance leader against the Japanese. Beginning in 1927, China was embroiled in a brutal civil war between the nationalist forces led by Chiang Kai-shek and the Mao led communists. As the Japanese conquered and occupied coastal Manchuria and coastal regions of China, the nationalists and communists formed a temporary anti-Japanese alliance in 1937. The most successful action Mao led against the Japanese was known as the "Hundred Regiments Campaign," where Chinese communists attacked Japanese positions in five provinces, leaving 20,000 dead.

## When Was Chiang Kai-shek Born?

Chiang Kai-shek, the leader of the Chinese Nationalist forces (Kuomintang) during the Chinese Civil War (1931-1937; 1945-1949), was born on October 31, 1887 in Xikou, China to a prosperous family. He pursued a military career from an early age and developed nationalist ideas due to seeing Chinese port cities being controlled by foreigners, which he attributed to the weakness of the Manchurian dominated Qin Dynasty. He eventually gained control of the Nationalist Party, known as the Kuomintang, and engaged Mao Zedong and his communist forces in a bloody war for control of China. Chiang and Mao declared a truce during World War II to fight the Japanese, though, and Chiang was the nominal head of government during that time. After the war, the Civil War began again and Mao's forces got the upper hand, forcing Chiang and his army to flee to the island of Formosa (Taiwan), which is where he died on May 20, 1948.

## Who Was Tokyo Rose?

There were actually several Tokyo Roses during World War II. The name was actually used by Allied troops in the Pacific Theater of the war for the many different English language female radio broadcasters the Japanese used for propaganda purposes. The women broadcasters would talk of the strength of the Japanese military in the hopes that it would demoralize the Allied servicemen. Only one of these women, Iva Toguri, was tried for her role as Tokyo Rose, although the case was far from clear. Toguri was an American citizen of Japanese descent who made the mistake of visiting Japan just before the Pearl Harbor attack. The situation left her stuck in Japan with no resources, so to make ends meet she took a job at a radio station doing English language broadcasts. She was convicted of treason in 1949, served six years in prison, but was later pardoned by President Gerald Ford in 1977 when it emerged that witnesses at her trial gave perjured testimony.

## What Was the Most Widely Used Tank by the Japanese during the War?

The Type 95 Ha Go was the most widely produced and used tank by the Japanese. The Type 95 Ha Go was a light tank that was first produced in 1936 and used heavily in Manchuria and China. Light most light tanks of the era, the Type 95 Ha Go was used primarily for infantry support and performed poorly against medium and heavy tanks, which were equipped with heavier weapons and more armor. The Type 95 Ha Go tank, though, was perfect for the Japanese Army, which usually fought in confined spaces such as in the Pacific islands, in dense jungles and forests in southeast Asia, or against foes with little armor as in China. Nearly 2,5000 Type 95 Ha Go tanks were produced until 1943.

## What Was the Kenpeitai?

The Kenpeitai was the Japanese military police and although in existence since 1881, it played a much more central role during World War II. In the occupied territories, the

Kenpeitai worked to squash anti-Japanese dissent and keep order behind the lines. Like its counterpart the SS in Germany, the Kenpeitai also had a secret police division, which engaged in espionage as well as domestic spying.

## Who Were Comfort Women?

Unfortunately, sexual exploitation has always been a major part of warfare. Throughout history, conquering armies have often seen it as their right to rape and sometimes kidnap the women of their enemies and World War II was no different. During World War II, when the Imperial Japanese Army was at the height of its power, it would routinely take women and girls from territories it occupied and force them to work in brothels, servicing Japanese soldiers. These women and girls forced into prostitution became known as "comfort women." Some scholars estimate that as many as 400,000 women and girls were forced to become comfort women during the war.

## Who Was the "Sky Samurai"?

Japanese ace pilot, sub-lieutenant Saburō Sakai (1916-2000) became known as the "Sky Samurai" during World War II due to his combat prowess. Sakai was born in Saga, Imperial Japan to a distinguished family with samurai ancestry, which influenced him to pursue a career in the military. He enrolled in the Imperial Navy at age sixteen and became a pilot in 1938, just in time for the Sino-Japanese War and World War II. Flying a Mitsubishi Zero, Sakai claimed between thirty and sixty aerial victories and became well-known among American pilots, who respected the Japanese ace's skills. Sakai was shot in the head by an American fighter at Guadalcanal, but miraculously returned to service in 1943 until the end of the war. After the war, Sakai became a Buddhist pacifist and later met some of the Americans he fought in the skies over the Pacific.

# EVENTS, GROUPS, AND PEOPLE IN EUROPE

## What Was the Madagascar Plan?

Although the Nazi Party platform held that Jews were inferior and would not be part of the Third Reich, there were a wide variety of opinions within the Party as to how that would be accomplished. The Madagascar Plan was the idea that once Germany had defeated France, it would send all of the Jews in Nazi occupied Europe to the French colony of Madagascar. The plan became popular with high ranking Nazis, but was abandoned due to British naval blockades and the idea of concentration camps becoming ascendant by 1942.

## When Were the First Concentration Camps Built?

The Konzentrationslager, known in English as "concentration camp," was perhaps the most notorious and well-known aspect of the Nazi regime. The Gestapo, which was the police wing of the SS, rounded up people considered to enemies of the Nazis and sent them to the camps where they were either forced to work or executed. The most infamous camps, such as Auschwitz and Treblinka, were built during the war and outside of Germany proper, but the Nazis wasted little time building camps after they came to power. The first camps were constructed after the official creation of the Gestapo on April 26, 1933. The early camps were spread throughout Germany, but there was a notable cluster in the northwest around the city of Osfriesland. Those sent to the early camps fit the same profile as those who were sent later: criminals, communists, Jews, homosexuals, and Roma/Gypsies.

## What Was the *Neuordnung*?

*Neuordnung* was the "New Order" over Europe that Nazi Germany was in charge of when it was at the zenith of its power in late 1942. Far beyond just a mere reordering of political boundaries, the idea of the New Order involved putting all of the Nazi Party's racial ideas into practice by forcibly moving, and if need be exterminating, populations throughout Europe. Berlin was envisioned to be the capital of not only Greater Germany, but also the economic nerve center of a continent wide common market that was tied to the Reichsmark. Germany's non-Germanic allies would be allowed nominal independence but the Slavic populations of eastern Europe would be either exterminated or pushed east, beyond the Ural Mountains. The vacuum caused by the displacement of the Slavic peoples would be filled with German settlers.

## When Was Heinrich Himmler Born?

Heinrich Luitpold Himmler was on October 7, 1900 in Munich, German Empire. Himmler was one of the Nazi Party's major theorists and philosophers and was the head of the *Schutzstaffel*/SS ("Protection Force"). As head of the SS, Himmler oversaw the arrest of the government's political enemies and the creation of the vast chain of prison and concentration camps. He fell out of favor with Hitler toward the end of the war, was captured by the British, and committed suicide while in prison on May 23, 1945.

## What Were the Einsatzgruppen?

The Einsatzgruppen, translated into English from German as "task forces," were SS death squads that patrolled the Eastern Front. The Einsatzgruppen generally operated behind the front lines to capture and kill the primary enemies of the Nazis, which included: partisans, Jews, communists, pre-war political leaders, and others known to be anti-fascist. It is believed that the group may have killed up to 2 million people during the war. After the war, many of the leaders of the Einsatzgruppen were tried with crimes against humanity and executed.

## What Were the German "Wolfpacks"?

When World War II began, Germany found itself at a great disadvantage on the seas. The British and French had a combined twenty-two battleships and eighty-three cruisers versus only three German "pocket" battleships. The *Kriegsmarine*, or German navy, built the massive battleship *Bismarck* to alleviate this problem, but it was sunk on its maiden voyage in May 1941. German admirals Erich Raeder and Karl Dönitz realized that the only way they could compete with the British navy was by using one of their successful tactics from World War I: U-boats. Technological innovations allowed World War II U-boats to hunt at night in groups, called wolfpacks, using radio. The wolfpacks sunk over 1,000 Allied ships in 1940 and 1,299 in 1941, reducing British exports to almost one-third of its pre-war total. The U-boat fleet peaked in 1942 with around 300 operational, which sank more than 2.6 million tons of Allied shipping materials that year.

## What European Countries Were Neutral during World War II?

Ireland, Spain, Sweden, Switzerland, and Portugal were neutral for the entire war, while Lithuania, Latvia, and Estonia declared their neutrality before the war, but were overrun by both the Soviets and Nazis at various times during the war. The "microstates" of Andorra, Liechtenstein, and Vatican City also remained neutral for the entire war. Each of the major neutral countries had its own reasons for neutrality and most continued diplomatic relations with both sides. Ireland had just achieved independence and was in no real position to engage in war, not to mention its population would have viewed allying with Britain most unfavorably. Switzerland had a long tradition of neutrality, as did Sweden, although both countries continued to do business with Germany. Portugal all but joined the Allies, but never did officially. Finally, Spain all but joined the Axis powers and even sent a volunteer division to the Eastern Front, but like Portugal never entered the war officially.

## What Role Did Rationing Play in the United Kingdom during the War?

Since the United Kingdom was an island nation and dependent on a large number of imports and since the Germans had essentially blockaded the British Isles with their U-boats, the British government was forced enact a nation-wide rationing system. During the beginning of the war, only gasoline was rationed, but as the war dragged on food, clothing, and cooking and heating oils were also rationed. Rationing was done through the Ministry of food, which issued coupon books to the citizens, which could then be redeemed at certain stores.

## Was Espionage Important in World War II?

Espionage played an extremely important role in World War II. Espionage, more commonly known as "spying", has been connected with military operations since ancient times. During World War II, spying became much more prevalent and expanded to include code making and codebreaking, sabotage, and infiltration of important industries. The Axis would often use bribes or appeals to fascist sympathizers in Allied nations in order to gather important information, while the Allies would identify highly placed individuals in Axis countries who were disaffected with their governments in order to "turn" them. In the end, the Soviets proved to be the masters of espionage as they stole the information from the Manhattan Project to develop their own nuclear weapons program.

## How Did Winston Churchill Become Prime Minister of the United Kingdom?

Winston Leonard Spencer Churchill (1874-1965) is best known for being Prime Minister of the United Kingdom/Great Britain during World War II and for delivering his "We shall never surrender" speech to the British people. After Germany's early battlefield successes, Chamberlin resigned as Prime Minister and conferred with King George VI and the leaders of the governments three major parties – the Liberals, Conservatives, and Labour – to make Churchill Prime Minster on May 10, 1940. Churchill was extremely popular during the war, walking among the people in the ruins of London and in the Tube during the Battle of Britain to help raise their spirits.

## Which Occupied Country Contributed the Most to Germany's War Effort?

France contributed the most to Germany's war effort with about 34,200,000 Reichsmarks by the end of the war. Of course, the French really had no choice in the matter, but the figure also include collaborating Vichy France. Since France is the largest country in continental western Europe the figure is partly to be expected, but France also has vast stretches of agricultural land that can feed the entire country. Although Italy was not technically occupied until late in the war, it was second, having contributed 13,300,000 Reichsmarks during the war.

## What Was Vichy France?

When Germany defeated France in 1940, the French decided to sign an armistice with the Germans. The agreement gave Germany direct control and occupation of northern France, including Paris, but control of southern France and Algeria was given to France's military marshal, Philippe Pétan. The capital of the new southern French government was in the city of Vichy, so the government became known as "Vichy France," as opposed to "Occupied France" or the "Free France" in exile. The Vichy government collaborated with the Nazis and helped carry out many of their policies in southern France. Although a number of Vichy officials were imprisoned and executed after the war, the French government awarded many amnesty in order to stabilize the government.

## What Was the National Council of the Resistance?

The National Council of the Resistance, or *Counseil National de la Résistance* as it was known in France, was the umbrella organization that coordinated and directed the different groups and individuals within the French resistance, in the north against the Germans and in the south against the Vichy government. Almost as soon as the Germans conquered and then occupied northern France, armed resistance, labor strikes, and other anti-Nazi activities ensued. Many of the groups and individuals taking part in the resistance were ideological dissimilar and ran the political spectrum from communist to fascist, so Charles de Gaulle, the leader of the French government in exile, established the National Council of the Resistance on May 23, 1943 to bring the groups together. Jean Moulin led operations on the ground until he was assassinated on July 8, 1943, but the organization continued until the end of the war.

## Who Were the Partisans in World War II?

The term "partisan" can be defined in a number of different ways, but in warfare it generally refers to someone who is violently resisting the foreign occupation of his or her country. More specifically in World War II it was generally used for the resistance groups in eastern Europe. Large pockets of resistance continued behind the front lines in Poland, the Soviet Union, and Yugoslavia throughout the war, with it being so effective in some places in Russia that some Soviet authority was even returned. Partisan attacks often brought brutal reprisals from the Germans, which were often carried out by the SS.

## What Was the Gestapo?

The Gestapo was the secret police of Nazi Germany. The Gestapo was originally formed from existing, non-political police agencies in Prussia, but was taken over by Himmler in 1934 and made part of the SS. The Gestapo had a wide range of duties and activities, both inside and outside of the Third Reich. Gestapo agents worked to weed out potentially disloyal Nazi Party members, as well as Germans with backgrounds considered counter to Nazi ideology: Jews, communists, and Gypsies just to name a few. In that capacity, the Gestapo oversaw the concentration camps. The Gestapo was also responsible for conducting espionage, surveillance, sabotage, and counter-intelligence operations as an intelligence agency.

## How Did a Muslim SS Division Come into Being?

It may seem ironic to many, or perhaps not, that the Nazis formed a predominately Muslim division of the Waffen SS. As the war on the Eastern Front began to bog down in late 1942, Heinrich Himmler came up with the idea to form volunteer Waffen SS divisions from the occupied territories throughout Europe. At first, most of these divisions were comprised of fascists and Nazi sympathizers from Germanic nations such as Norway, Denmark, and the Netherlands, but after awhile they began accepting prisoners of war and volunteers from France, Belgium, and even Britain. In early 1943, Himmler saw a new group that he believed could help—the Bosnian Muslims. The Bosnian Muslims traditionally hated the Serbs of the Balkans region, which the Axis powers were having a difficult time pacifying, so the Nazis decided to form young Muslim men into a division and use them along with the Croats of the fascist Ustashe to control the Balkans. Recruitment for the 13th Waffen Mountain Division of the SS Handschar began in 1943 and the division was put into the field in 1944 to carry out anti-partisan activities. Himmler, who was a pagan and believed that Christianity was weak, had no problem with a Muslim SS division and believed that the Bosnians were racially Aryans, descended from Germans and Iranians. The term "handschar" was derived from a traditional Ottoman sword. The Hanschar Division had unique uniforms that expressed their Muslim identity: they wore fez style hats and had an image of the handschar on their lapel.

## What Was Adolf Eichmann's Role in the Third Reich?

Adolf Eichmann (1906-1962) was a high ranking member of the Nazi Party and a member of the SS whose primary job was the deport Jews from German occupied territory, in order to carry out the "Final Solution." Early in the Third Reich, Eichmann tried to promote Jewish emigration policies such as the Madagascar Plan and by training Jews to be farmers in Palestine, but as the war dragged on most of his plans involved the expansion of the concentration camp system and the use of Europe's railroad system to deliver Jews to the camps. After the war, Eichmann lived under aliases, eventually fleeing to what he believed was the safety of Argentina, but he was captured by Israeli Mossad agents in a covert operation and brought to Israel where he was tried, convicted, and executed for crimes against the Jewish people.

## Why Did Hungary Join the Axis Powers?

Like most countries, Hungary was adversely affected by the Great Depression during the 1930s and as in Germany, the population began gravitating toward far-right and far-left political parties for answers. The far-right was more successful. Hungary developed deep economic ties with Nazi Germany and Fascist Italy by the mid-1930s and subsequently anti-Semitism became more institutionalized as the government tried to appease fascist groups such as the Arrow Cross Party, which were becoming more popular. Hungarian nationalists also had their own territorial ambitions, although quite modest when compared to the Germans, which all eventually led to the Kingdom of Hungary to join the Axis Powers on November 20, 1940. Hungarian soldiers fought in the Balkans and on the Eastern Front.

## What Was Finland's Status During World War II?

Of all the countries involved in World War II, Finland was perhaps the most interesting due to its unique status. Finns fought alongside Germans on the Eastern Front, but the Finish government was never an official Axis power. Due to the results of the Winter War, anti-Soviet sentiment was high in Finland and most Finns were eager to recover territory they lost by aligning with Germany against the Soviet Union on the Eastern Front. From June 25, 1941 until September 19, 1944 Finland was at war against the Soviet Union in what became known as the "Continuation War." Officially a co-belligerent with Nazi Germany against the Soviet Union, which brought German troops onto Finnish soil, Finland nevertheless retained its democratically elected government for the duration of the war. Finland signed an armistice with the Soviet Union, joined the Allies, and then fought against Germany in the "Lapland War" from September 19, 1944 until the end of World War II in 1945.

## Who Was Léon Degrelle?

Léon Degrelle (June 15, 1906-March 31, 1994) was a Belgian fascist who became famous for collaborating with the Nazis during World War II by leading a foreign division of the Waffen SS on the Eastern Front. Degrelle was an ethnic Walloon (French speaking Belgian), who gravitated toward right-wing causes and eventually fascism in the years before World War II. After the war began, the Belgian government arrested Degrelle on suspicion of collaborating with the Germans and sent him to France, but he was released when the Germans conquered France. Degrelle later joined a newly formed volunteer detachment of Walloonian SS and fought on the Eastern Front, where he distinguished himself enough to be awarded the battlefield decoration of the Iron Cross. After the war Degrelle fled to Franco's Spain where he lived until his death. He was a public figure in Spain and was an outspoken and unrepentant fascist.

## When Did Bulgaria Join the Axis Powers?

The Kingdom of Bulgaria officially joined the Axis Powers on March 1, 1941 when it signed the Tripartite Pact. As one of the losing countries in World War I, Bulgaria lost some of its land in the treaties that were signed after the war. In the years between the war, Bulgaria, like many other countries in Europe, experienced a surge in nationalist populism, bringing a government to power that was willing to side with Germany to get some of its lost land back. Bulgarian troops fought alongside German and Italian troops in the Balkans, but not on the Eastern Front. A communist coup toppled the nationalist Bulgarian government in September 1944, which then officially changed sides, declaring war against Germany.

## What Role Did Propaganda Play in World War II?

Propaganda played an incredibly important role in World War II for both the Axis and Allies, more so than any previous war, largely due to improvements in technology and increases in global literacy. Since most people in the industrialized world could read when World War II began, the creation of propaganda posters became a ubiquitous part of life in most countries during the war. There were two basic types of propaganda posters: those that demonized the enemy and those that exhorted non-combatants, usually women, to support the home front. Hollywood also played an important role by producing films that supported the American war effort.

## Who Was Axis Sally?

Axis Sally was the name given to two different American women—Mildred Gillars (1900-1988) and Rita Zucca (1912-1998)—who broadcast pro-Axis English language shows via radio during World War II. Gillars was an American born woman who began broadcasting a pro-Nazi radio show titled *Home Sweet Home* in 1942. Zucca was an American born woman of Italian ancestry who traveled to Italy to visit family before the war, but began broadcasting a radio show similar to Gillars' in 1943. Both women were arrested and tried for their participation with the Axis powers after the war. Since Zucca renounced her American citizenship, only the post-Fascist Italian authorities tried her, giving her a four-and-a-half year sentence for collaboration, for which she served nine months. Gillars was convicted of one count of treason in 1949, sentenced to up to thirty years in prison, and was released in 1961.

## Who Was Lord Haw-Haw?

American born Irishman William Joyce (1906-1946) was known as Lord Haw-Haw during World War II. Joyce was born in the United States to an Irish Catholic father and a Unionist Protestant mother, which seemingly set the tone for his life of being on two sides at once. He was briefly a member of the BUF but was actually expelled by Mosely for being too violent and radical, which put him on the list to be arrested by the British government under Defence Regulation 18B, so he fled to Germany in 1939. During the war, Joyce worked for the Nazis broadcasting English language, pro-Nazi propaganda via the radio under the pseudonym "Lord Haw-Haw," but later used his real name. After the war, he was captured by the British near Denmark, sent back to England to be tried for treason, was convicted, and executed by hanging.

# CHAPTER 4:

# THE TIDE TURNS

## PEOPLE

### What Was the Infamy Speech?

On December 8, 1941, the day after the Japanese attack on Pearl Harbor, American President Franklin Delano Roosevelt gave a speech to a joint session of Congress where he said December 7 would be a "date which will live in infamy." The speech was just over seven minutes long but had the effect of rallying the American people for the war effort.

### When Was Douglas MacArthur Born?

Douglas MacArthur was born on January 26, 1880 in Little Rock, Arkansas. MacArthur came from a military family, attended and graduated from West Point, and served in World War I, which is where he earned his reputation for bravery and a keen military mind. He retired from the U.S. Army in 1937, but was recalled into service by President Roosevelt in 1941 as a major general and then as a lieutenant general. After overseeing the U.S. withdrawal from the Philippines in early 1942, he returned in July 1944 as he said he would. MacArthur died a five star general on April 5, 1964 at the age of eighty-four.

## When Was Georgy Zhukov Born?

Georgy Konstantinovich Zhukov was born on December 1, 1896 in the Russian Empire. Zhukov served honorably during World War I for the tsar, but joined the Bolsheviks and moved up quickly through the ranks during the Russian Civil War. He eventually became the Marshal of the Soviet Union after having successfully defended Moscow in late 1941 and early 1942. General Zhukov played a major role in the Soviet Union's counteroffensive and the Battle of Berlin in early 1945.

## What Role Did American Women Play in World War II?

American women, like women from all of the major countries involved in World War II, played important roles in the home front and in support within the military. With most of the young, healthy men drafted, munitions and military assembly factories needed women to fill the void. A nationwide call was put out for women to work in these factories, which is perhaps best personified by the propaganda poster of Rosie the Riveter saying "We Can Do It!" Although combat was not an option for women in World War II, tens of thousands American women also served in the Army's Women's Army Auxiliary Corps (WAAC) in administrative positions and as nurses.

## How Did Bernard Montgomery Become Field Marshal of the British Forces?

Bernard Law Montgomery (1887-1976) was a career officer in the British Army and one of the major Allied military leaders during World War II. Montgomery began his military career in 1908 and served with distinction on the Western Front during Word War I. Between the wars, "Monty" as he was often called, worked his way up the ranks and was given command of the 3$^{rd}$ Division of the British Expeditionary Force, which acquitted itself well during the fall of France. Montgomery, though, cemented his reputation as a supreme military commander when he was given command of the Eight Army in North Africa in August 1942. He defeated Rommel and the Afrika Korps at the Second Battle of El-Alamein, which ended the Germans' and Italians' thrust toward Egypt and gave the Allies a much needed morale boost. Although Montgomery played a crucial role in the planning and execution of Operation Overlord (the Allied invasion of Normandy), American General Dwight D. Eisenhower was appointed Supreme Commander of the Allied forces. British and American political leaders thought that since the majority of the Allied forces on the Western Front were Americans, that they should be led by an American general. Montgomery was upset with the decision as he believed he was a better general than Eisenhower, so as a consolation Prime Minister Churchill made him Field Marshal of all British forces on September 1, 1944.

## When Was General Patton Born?

General George Smith Patton Junior was born on November 11, 1885 in San Gabriel, California to George Senior and Ruth Patton. As a young man, Patton was athletic but never much of an academic. He was admitted to and graduated from the United State Military Academy at West Point, New York and participated in the 1916 expedition to capture Mexican rebel Pancho Villa. He served in World War I primarily in an administrative role at first, but became acquainted with tanks and began teaching tank tactics. Patton eventually saw action and was wounded in battle in September 1918. After the war, Patton was assigned to the cavalry, which by then had transitioned from horses to tanks, and steadily moved up in rank to colonel. When World War II began it became clear to the government that tanks would play a key role in the war, so

Patton was promoted to general due to his success leading tank units and his understanding of tank warfare. He won several battles in North Africa and Italy, earning him the nickname "old blood and guts," and played a key role at Normandy and the Battle of the Bulge. Patton was involved in a car accident after the war in Germany on December 8, 1945 and died in a hospital in Heidelberg on December 21, 1945 at the age of sixty.

## Who Was Otto Skorzeny?

Otto Skorzeny (1908-1975) was lieutenant colonel in the Waffen SS who led many different commando missions for Germany, most notably the rescue of Benito Mussolini from an alpine hotel on September 12, 1943. Recognizable for a large scare across his left check that he received in a fencing match before the war, Skorzeny's missions were often mythologized and sometimes exaggerated by his supporters and enemies alike. Since he was a member of the Waffen, which was the military wing of the SS, Skorzeny had nothing to do with the concentration camps, although he did face war crimes charges for leading a commando raid during the Battle of the Bulge where he and his men dressed in Allied uniforms. While awaiting trial, he escaped from prison in 1948, fled to the safety of Spain, and lived and worked in Egypt and Argentina for several years. Although he was declared "denazified" by the West German government in 1952, he continued to live in Spain until his death.

## When Was Admiral Nimitz Born?

Admiral Chester William Nimitz was born on February 24, 1885 in Fredericksburg, Texas to Chester Bernhard and Anna Nimitz. His father died before he was born so he was partly raised by his German born paternal grandfather, who was a former merchant sailor and Texas Ranger. Nimitz graduated from the United States Naval Academy in 1905 and then went on to a lifelong career in the United States Navy. He served in World War I, but it was after the war when he began to make his mark on the Navy, commanding destroyers and submarines and also conducting experiments on underwater refueling. Days after the Japanese attack on Pearl Harbor, President Roosevelt selected Nimitz to be commander-in-chief of the Pacific Fleet and promoted him to the rank of admiral. After successfully leading fleet in the Pacific, Nimitz was promoted to fleet admiral in 1944 and was the American representative when the Japanese signed their official, unconditional surrender. Admiral Chester Nimitz died on February 20, 1966 in California at the age of eighty.

## Who Was Hanna Reitsch?

Hanna Reitsch (1912-1979) was a pioneer in aviation, as she was the first woman in history to pilot a helicopter, a jet airplane, and a rocket. She was born and raised in what was Prussia, but is today Poland and as a young woman pushed the boundaries of many gender stereotypes of the time by first studying medicine and then becoming heavily involved in aviation. Reitsch was an ardent believer in the Nazi cause, having worked with the party by first doing modeling for propaganda posters and later by helping develop experimental aircraft. Toward the end of the war she was captured by the Americans, imprisoned for a short time, and went through the "denazification" process. She later worked for the West German government in the African nation of Ghana.

## Who Were the Main Scientists in the Manhattan Project?

The Manhattan Project was the United States Army program that developed the first nuclear weapons, which were later used on Japan. The program began in 1942 and was fairly decentralized, with scientists working in labs in Oak Ridge, Tennessee, Los Alamos, New Mexico, and Utah, as well as several smaller labs at other locations around the country. Major General Leslie Groves (1896-1970) of the Army Corps of Engineers oversaw the program, gathering some of the world's best engineers, physicists, mathematicians, and other scientists, which included Robert Oppenheimer (1904-1967), Stanislaw Ulam (1909-1984), Stafford L. Warren (1896-1981), Kenneth Bainbridge (1904-1996), and Joan Hinton (1921-2010) among others. Hinton was one of the few female scientists who worked on the project.

## How Did Eisenhower Become the Supreme Commander of the Allied Force in Europe?

Dwight David Eisenhower (1890-1969) was a career military officer who had no combat experience before World War II. Despite his lack of wartime experience, which earned him the enmity of some of his peers, he had a keen strategic and political mind. In late 1942, Eisenhower was appointed as the Supreme Commander Allied Expeditionary Force of the North African Theater of Operations, where he led his troops successfully, eventually invading Italy. Pleased with his success in North Africa, Roosevelt chose Eisenhower to be the Supreme Allied Commander in Europe over General George Marshall and General Montgomery. Prime Minister Churchill concurred, believing that since the Americans comprise the majority of the troops that would invade Europe an American general should be given command of the entire army.

## Who Ran the Lucy Spy Ring?

It is believed that German national Rudolf Roessler (1897-1958) ran the spy ring from a publishing firm in Switzerland. In the years just before World War II, Roessler was approached by Wehrmacht officers unhappy with Hitler and Nazi rule in

Germany. They proposed a system whereby they would give Roessler intelligence about the Germany Army, which he would then send to the Soviets, usually via Swiss agents. Ten German officers and politicians were part of the ring along with Roessler and five other Swiss agents.

## In What Branches of Service Did African-Americans Serve?

Black Americans served in all branches of the military during World War II (the Air Force was still part of the Army) in varying roles. Because the military was segregated until 1948, black sailors almost always worked in support roles at the bases. The Army had several black combat units and divisions, including: the 92nd Infantry Division (Buffalo Soldiers); the 93rd Infantry Division; and the 332nd Fighter Group (Tuskegee Airmen). Black women also served in the military in clerical and administrative roles and as nurses.

## When Was Charles de Gaulle Born?

Charles de Gaulle was born on November 22, 1890 in Lille, France. He was a World War I veteran, officer in the French army, and early proponent of armored warfare. After France was defeated and occupied by Germany, de Gaulle retreated to England where he organized the French Resistance and led the French government in exile. His efforts during the war made him extremely popular in France, helping him win the presidency in 1959, which he held until 1969. He died at his home from a ruptured blood vessel on November 9, 1970 at the age of eighty.

## Who Was Lydia Litvyak?

Lydia Litvyak (1921-1943) was a Soviet fighter pilot who was the first female pilot to shoot down an enemy plane during

World War II. Known as the "White Rose of Stalingrad," Litvyak began flying as a teenager and joined the female 586th Fighter Aviation Regiment of the Red Army after the war began, flying a YAK-1 fighter. She was later transferred to a men's squadron where she became an ace, claiming between eight and twelve individual kills. Litvayk was shot down over the city of Kursk during Operation Citadel and was presumed killed on August 1, 1943.

# ON THE BATTLEFIELD: EUROPEAN THEATER

## What Impact Did the Battle of Britain Have on the War?

From July 10, 1940 until October 31, 1940, the German air force, or *Luftwaffe*, sent wave after wave of bomber and fighter planes to attack southern England in order to prepare for the amphibious invasion of Britain, known as "Operation Sea Lion." The first two months of the battle was almost totally comprised of air battles, with the British Royal Air Force (RAF) winning the day. The Germans lost 1,733 aircraft during that time and were reduced to just 273 versus 732 RAF planes by October 1. The Luftwaffe changed its tactics in mid-September by targeting civilian targets in what became known as the "Blitz," hoping that the British would sue for peace. Although the Blitz killed more than 42,000 civilians, the Germans clearly lost the Battle of Britain and had to cancel Operation Sea Lion. As a result, the Germans lost a good chunk of their air force and the British were able to stay in the war until the end.

## When Was the German Battleship *Bismarck* Sunk?

The *Bismarck* was sunk on May 27, 1941 by a British squadron of an aircraft carrier, two battleships, three cruisers, and six destroyers. The *Bismarck* was a state of the art German battleship commissioned in August 1940. After leaving with a squadron on a mission to the north Atlantic on May 5, the *Bismarck* became involved in the Battle of the Denmark Strait on May 24. The ship then sailed into the Atlantic where it was far from air support, but nearly got away from the British ships before being spotted off the French coast. Only 110 of the *Biskmarck's* 2,200 crew survived. Both Admiral Günther Lütjens (1889-1941) and Captain Ernst Lindemann (1894-1941) went down with the *Bismarck* on May 27.

## How Did Stalin's Five Year Plans Help the Soviet Union's Ability to Wage War?

As much as Stalin's Five Year Plans hurt the Soviet Union before and during the early stages of the war, they helped in the later stages. Once the Soviet Union received much needed supplies from the Allies through Iran and the Pacific, they were able to focus on industrial production. Although the early Five Year Plans hurt the Soviet Union's agriculture, it laid the foundations for a strong industrial base. Stalin's Five Year Plans transformed sleepy towns in the Ural Mountains, such as Sverdlovsk and Chelyabinsk, into industrial giants, which proved to be vital later in the war because they were out of range of German bombers.

## How Did the Office of Strategic Services Form?

The Office of Strategic Services (OSS) was the predecessor of the American Central Intelligence Agency. Before World War II, the United States had no official intelligence agency, so when the war began most intelligence functions were handled by the military with assistance from the British. After the British trained a number of potential agents, the OSS was officially formed by executive order from President Roosevelt on June 13, 1942. The OSS was active in both the Pacific and

European theaters of war, gathering intelligence and working with partisans behind enemy lines.

## When Was the Enigma Machine Decrypted?

The enigma machine was a complicated mechanical and electrical device that the Germans used to send and receive coded messages. The machine was first invented in 1918 by Arthur Scherbius and was quickly picked up by the military as useful tool for sending and receiving messages. Almost as soon as the machine began being used, efforts were under way to decrypt it. Polish scientists made the first serious attempts to decrypt Enigma using a counter electro-mechanical device known as a "bombe." The British built their own bombe and were routinely decrypting Enigma messages by 1941. The Germans countered by making more complex Enigma machines, but once the United States entered the war the U.S. Navy and Army built their own, more complex bombes that were able to break most German cyphers by 1943.

## How Did the Jeep First Enter the War?

The military vehicle known as the Jeep was American made, but the first models were sent to the Soviet Union in early 1941. The creation of the Jeep came in 1940 when the American Bantam Car Company and the Willys-Overland Company were contracted by the United States Army to build a prototype of a four-wheeled drive reconnaissance and service car. Although the Bantam Car Company created the first model, the United States army gave the designs to Willys-Overland and the Ford Motor Company. Willys-Overland came up with the MB model, which became the standard Jeep model from that point forward. Willys-Overland accepted a non-exclusive license for the Jeep during the war to allow

Ford to produced their own version. Of the more than 600,000 Jeeps produced during World War II, about 30% were sent to the British and Soviet armies. Willys-Overland trademarked the Jeep name in 1943 and began production of a civilian model in 1945.

## What Was the Most Effective Soviet Tank in the War?

The T-34 was without question the most capable and effective Soviet tank during World War II. Considered a "medium" tank because it had more armor and firepower than a light tank, but less armor than a heavy tank, even famed German tank commander Heinz Guderian was impressed with the tank, noting that it was superior to any German panzer early in the war. Designed by engineer Mikhail Koshkin, the T-34 began hitting the battlefield in 1940 and by the end of the war more than 80,000 were produced.

## What Was the "Great Patriotic War"?

The Great Patriotic War was the name Stalin gave to the Soviet Union's fight against Germany and the other Axis powers on the Eastern Front of World War II. Historically and ideologically speaking, communists shunned nationalism and patriotism, seeing themselves instead as warriors in an international class war that knew no state boundaries. In practice, Stalin and the leaders of the Communist Party in the Soviet Union knew that standard Marxist and communist slogans and ideology would motivate the people to fight the invasion far less than appeals to red-blooded patriotism, so the term "Great Patriotic War" was adopted for propaganda purposes.

## What Was Operation Torch?

Operation Torch was the first major Allied military offensive against Germany in World War II by the British and Americans from November 8 through November 16, 1941. The operation was a major invasion of Algeria and Morocco in North Africa, which was intended to drive the Vichy French from the region and establish an Allied base for the later invasion of Italy. Led by American General Dwight D. Eisenhower, Operation Torch marked the beginning of the end for the Vichy French government, gave the Allies a moral and logistical boost, and established Eisenhower as a capable military commander.

## What Was the Result of the Battle of Stalingrad?

The Battle of Stalingrad, which took place in the Soviet city of Stalingrad, was one of the longest and most important battles in World War II. From August 23, 1942 to February 2, 1943, the Germans and their allies laid siege to the strategically important industrial city of Stalingrad (now Volgograd), in what became the most destructive battle in human history. Both sides sent over a million men into the field and almost as many died when the smoke cleared. Great destruction was done to the city and it was almost entirely depopulated, but the Red Army enacted a crushing defeat on the Axis powers. The Soviets were on the offensive from that point on in the Eastern Front and Germany's allies were all but knocked out of the war.

## What Was Operation Husky?

Operation Husky was the codename for the Allied invasion of Sicily that took place from July 9 through August 17, 1943. The Allies had been working their way through the Axis forces in North Africa since 1941 with the long-term goal of invading Italy, which would open a second front in Europe. The Allies hoped that the invasion of Italy would take the Italians out of the war and force the Germans to take units from the Eastern Front in order to prevent the collapse of Mussolini's fascist regime. Although the fighting was fierce, the Allies were able to take the island of Sicily due to their overwhelming numbers. The victory did as exactly as the Allies had hoped—Mussolini's regime collapsed and Hitler was forced to take troops from the Eastern Front to defend German occupied Italy and the Balkans.

## When Was the United States' First Airborne Division Created?

The existing 82$^{nd}$ Infantry Division became the first American airborne division when it was changed to the 82$^{nd}$ Airborne Division on August 15, 1942. The idea of parachuting soldiers behind enemy lines was a new concept in World War II and first heavily utilized by the Germans on the Western Front in 1940. After Germany's successful invasion of Crete in May and June 1941, the Wehrmacht used paratroopers far less and never again *en masse*. The Allies began developing paratrooper divisions with Major General Mathew Ridgeway commanding the United States first paratrooper division, the 82$^{nd}$ Airborne. The 82$^{nd}$ Airborne first saw action in Operation Husky and Anzio and then went on to play an important role in the Normandy invasion. The 82$^{nd}$ Airborne conducted four division jumps and had 1,619 of its men killed in action.

## When Did the Warsaw Ghetto Uprising Take Place?

When the Germans conquered and then occupied Poland, they immediately began rounding up their political and racial enemies. Many were sent to concentration camps but in areas with high densities of Jews, such as Warsaw, they were crowded into already existing Jewish neighborhoods, known as ghettos. As the situation in the Warsaw ghetto became desperate, and Jews there learned that the Germans were in retreat on all fronts, an uprising was organized that took place on April 19, 1943. The uprising was brutally suppressed, with nearly all inhabitants being killed or sent to concentration camps.

## When Was Operation Citadel?

Operation Citadel, the last major German offensive on the Eastern Front, took place from July 5 to July 17, 1943. After being defeated at Stalingrad, the Germans attempted to launch a major offensive/counter attack near the Russian city of Kursk. The German plan was to move on Kursk from a northern and a southern salient, surround the city, and destroy the Red Army units in the area, thereby allowing for a new offensive toward Stalingrad and/or Moscow. Soviet intelligence learned about the German operation, but instead of attacking the German position first, Soviet General Zhukov ordered the Red Army to dig in and assume a more defensive posture. Although the Germans continually moved forward and won most of the battles during the offensive, they did not have the manpower to win a battle of attrition. After the Western Allies had initiated Operation Husky in Sicily, Hitler feared that southern Europe was too exposed so Operation Citadel was cancelled to allow troops to be sent to Italy.

## Who Built the P-51 Mustang Fighters?

The American aerospace corporation North American Aviation developed and began production of the Mustang in the summer of 1940. The Mustangs were first used by the British Royal Air Force (RAF), where they proved to be quite effective during the last week of the Battle of Britain. Once the

United States entered the war, the Mustang helped the Allies gain air supremacy in the European Theater of operations.

## Why Did the Allies Land at Anzio?

The Battle of Anzio, Italy, which lasted from January 22 to June 5, 1944, was a battle that although the Allies won, but it came at great loss of life. The purpose was to flank the heavy fortifications known as the "Gustav Line" that German General Albert Kesselring had built across Italy south of Rome. Anzio was deemed to be a suitable beachhead north of the Gustav Line where Allied forces could land, encircle the Axis forces, and end the war in Italy relatively quick. The Anzio landing was oversaw by American Major General John P. Lucas, who initially only sent two infantry divisions to the beachhead with no armor support. Lucas' passivity has been seen as one of the reasons why the Battle of Anzio took so long and was so costly, but Kesselring later said in Lucas' defense that the Allied plan was flawed to begin with and they also failed to take into account the desperate nature of the German forces.

## What Were Some of the Beaches Besides Omaha the Allies Stormed on D-Day?

D-Day is the term often used to refer to the Allied invasion/landing on Normandy, France on June 6, 1944. Codenamed Operation Neptune, it was and remains the largest amphibious military invasion in world history. Americans are most familiar with the landing on the beach codenamed Omaha due to its portrayal in films and other popular media, but there were four other beaches where the Allies landed: Utah, Sword, Gold, and Juno. Americans also landed at Utah, while the British landed at Gold and Sword, and the Canadians landed at Juno.

## When Were Jet Airplanes First Used in Combat?

The Germans began experimenting with jet aircraft before the war, creating the Heinkel He 178 as the world's first turbo jet airplane when it successfully flew a test on September 1, 1939. Although the plane was a success and the Luftwaffe continued to develop more jets during the war, most of the Wehrmacht's resources went toward the army and more conventional types of aircraft. The first jet plane to see combat in World War II was the German Messerschmitt ME 262, which flew its first combat mission in June 1944. The first Allied jet to see combat was the British Gloster Meteor in July 1944. The Americans also flew a jet in combat in World War II; the Lockheed P-80 Shooting Star first saw action as reconnaissance planes over Italy in early 1945. The only Since jets were used so late in the war, they had little impact on the outcome, although many models were built during World War II were in operation for several decades.

## How Did the Siegfried Line Get Its Name?

When the French began building the Maginot Line during the 1930, the Germans countered by building a series of border fortifications along their western border with France, Belgium, and the Netherlands they called the *Westwall*, or West Wall. In the English speaking world, the fortifications were known as the "Siegfried Line" for the mythological German hero, Siegfried, whose skin only had one small vulnerable point. The Siegfried Line was largely abandoned for most of the war, but was reactivated after the Allied D-day Invasion on 19 June 1944. In August 1944, there were over 24,000 American casualties along the Siegfried Line. The Germans would use the defensive positions to launch their last major offensive in the west, the Battle of Bulge, in December 1944.

## What Was the Most Widely Use Allied Medium Tank during World War II?

The American Medium Tank 4 Sherman, simply known as the "Sherman," was the most used medium tank by the Allies. The Sherman, which was named for Civil War Union General and American President William T. Sherman, was produced from February 1942 until the end of the war. Nearly 50,000 Shermans were made and not only used by the Americans, but also the Soviets and British. As a medium tank, the Sherman had lighter armor than some of the larger German tanks, such as the Tiger, but was much more maneuverable. Although the Sherman was used in both theaters of the World War II, the small islands and jungles of the Pacific Theater often relegated the Sherman in favor of light tanks and infantry.

## How Did Operation Market-Garden Get Its Name?

Operation Market Garden was Field Marshal Montgomery's plan to quickly capture nine bridges across the Rhine River in the Netherlands using paratroopers, which would allow Allied armor divisions to more easily invade Germany. The operation's codename was derived from the bridges being "Market," which would be taken first by the paratrooper divisions, while "Garden" was in reference to the armored and regular infantry that would follow. Operation Market-Garden was launched on September 17, 1944, involved over 40,000 paratroopers—including the American Army's 101st and 82nd Airborne Units—and ended in Allied defeat a week and a day later. The failure meant that the Allies would later have to confront the Germany Army directly at the Siegfried Line.

**When Was the Battle of the Bulge?**

The Battle of the Bulge took place from December 16, 1944 until January 25, 1945. Perhaps somewhat ironically, most of the battle took place in the Ardennes Forest, which is where Germany began its invasion of France four-and-a-half years prior. The Battle of the Bulge is also known as the Ardennes Counteroffensive because it was Germany's last counteroffensive on the Western Front. The German strategy called for a quick strike from the Siegfried Line to the Atlantic, which would cut Allied forces in Belgium and the Netherlands off from the rest of the army. It was a desperation move that if successful, could possibly buy Germany time on the Eastern Front and/or be leverage for a more favorable surrender to the western Allies. The initial thrust was successful, but the heavy losses on both sides were too much for the Germans. The Allied victory cleared the way for the march to Germany, all but destroying the German military on the Western Front.

**How Much Did the United Kingdom's Colonies Contribute to the War Effort?**

More than 6.5 million British men fought in World War II and nearly 250,000 were killed, but the numbers are much higher when the colonies are included. A total of nearly 400,000 British *and* colonial soldiers were killed in World War II, including 39,000 Canadians, 24,000 Indians, 10,000 New Zealanders, 7,000 South Africans, and 30,000 from Australia and other colonies. Colonials fought in all theaters of World War II, which included 15,000 colonial seamen in the merchant navy. The merchant navy was crucial in its efforts to bring provisions to the island nation. There is little doubt that Great Britain/the United Kingdom would not have been so successful in the war without its colonial support.

## Why Was Leningrad Never Captured by the Axis Forces?

Leningrad, now known as St. Petersburg, was a major target for the Germans during World War II because it was the Soviet Union's second largest city, was the center of the Bolshevik Revolution, and was home to the Soviet Union's major Baltic Sea port. German Army Group A, led by Field Marshall Wilhelm Ritter von Leeb (1876-1956), cut all roads and rail lines east, south, and west of the city while the Finnish Army, led by Field Marshall Carl Mannerheim, cut off all routes to the north beginning on September 8, 1941. A more than two year siege then took place that finally ended on January 27, 1944 with an Axis retreat. The Soviets suffered more than three million military casualties and more than half of its civilian population of 650,000 was lost, although most were evacuated. The situation was dire, with civilians resorting to cannibalism toward the end of the siege. A number of factors, though, played a role in Leningrad being able to survive. The Finns played more of a defensive role and did not actively participate in the actual siege operations other than seizing roads and railways. The Red Army knew that it was a fight to the death and that the Germans would offer them no quarter if they surrendered. Finally, as the situation changed in other parts of the Eastern Front, the Soviets were able to launch a counteroffensive to lift the siege.

## What Role Did the Weather and Geography Play on the Eastern Front?

Russia has been described at different points in world history as a sleeping giant, due to a combination of its size and difficulty to conquer. Since the thirteenth century, Russia has been invaded numerous times, but rarely occupied for very long. The Mongols had the best success occupying Russia, partly because they came from the east, but every modern

European invasion of Russia ended in disaster. Charles XII of Sweden's invasion of Russia in 1709 and Napoleon's invasion in 1812 were foiled due to the cold weather and immensity of the country. When the Germans invaded the Soviet Union in 1941, they thought that the war would be over quickly, but they too made some of the same mistakes. After trudging through the Pripet Marshes in Belarus, the Germans were faced with the logistical problems of overextended supply lines and having to build airstrips. The delays allowed the Soviets to move their war factories east of the Ural Mountains where they were safe from German bombers. It also allowed them to raise more recruits from Siberia. Finally, the cold Russian winters hampered the ability of the Germans to use their planes and the freezing temperatures often froze the fuel lines on German tanks and mechanized vehicles.

## What Was the Most Produced Combat Aircraft during World War II?

36,183 units of the Soviet Ilyushin Il-2 were built along with 6,166 units of its successor, the Ilyushin Il-10, to make it the most produced military aircraft during the war. The Ilyushin was named for its designer, Sergey Ilyushin, who envisioned an air to surface bomber to support infantry. Production of the Ilyushians lagged early in the war as Germany won battle after battle, continually moving east, but once the Soviets went on the offensive after Stalingrad production was drastically increased and by the time the Red Army made it to Berlin the Ilyushins were free to bomb German infantry, artillery, and panzers at will.

## When Was the Dnieper-Carpathian Offensive?

The Dnieper-Carpathian Offensive took place from December 24 1943 to April 17, 1944. The Soviet offensive began at the Dnieper River in Ukraine, spearheading the Axis lines into the

Carpathian Mountains in Romania, and ended with a complete victory for the Red Army. The Germans and their Romanian allies lost over a quarter million men in the offensive and hundreds of tanks, planes, and artillery pieces. Although the Germans regrouped and stabilized the front line once more, they only were able to do so by drawing away tanks and planes from western Europe, which aided in the Western Allies success at Normandy. The Dnieper-Carpathian Offensive decimated the Romanian infantry, which led to leaders of that country entering into secret negotiations to surrender to the Soviets.

## What Was the Wolfsschanze?

The *Wolfsschanze*, which translates from German into English as "Wolf's Lair," was Adolf Hitler's first military headquarters in the Eastern Front. Located outside of the Prussian town of Rastenburg (now in Poland), the Wolf's Lair was built in 1941 just before Operation Barbarossa. Due to the changing fortunes of the Germany Army and the need to keep Hitler safe, several other headquarters were also used as front military headquarters during the war. The Wolf's Lair was the location of the ill-fated assassination attempt on July 20, 1944. The SS responded to the assassination attempt by killing not only the military officers who were involved, but most of their associates and some of their family members.

## What Impact Did the V-2 Rocket Have on World War II

The German *Vergeltungswaffe 2*, which translates into English as "Vengeance Weapon 2," was a state of the art guided ballistic missile the Germans began using in June 1944. Developed by Wernher von Braun and other scientists, the V-2 was a major improvement on the earlier V-2 rocket because the guidance system was more precise and it was the first type of rocket to enter space. Although V-2 rocket attacks killed over 9,000 people and did significant damage to some cities, namely Antwerp and London, they failed to stop or even slow down the Allied advance on Germany. The V-2's true impact came after the war when Braun and other rocket scientists surrendered to the Western Allies and then helped start NASA. The Soviets also captured a number of German rocket scientists who helped develop the Soviet space program.

**How Did Mussolini Die?**

Benito Mussolini was executed on April 28, 1945 by anti-Fascist Italian partisans. After the Allied invasion of Italy in August 1943, Mussolini's government collapsed and he was reduced to being ruler over a northern Italian puppet state known as Italian Social Republic. As the Allies continued to work their way north up the Italian peninsula, Italian partisans, who were primarily members of the Communist Party, got involved and began actively searching for Mussolini. On April 27, 1945, the partisans capture Mussolini and his mistress, Claretta Petacci, as they were trying to escape in a convoy to Switzerland. The Leader, Petacci, and other capture Italian Fascists were shot and then hung upside down in the public square in Milan.

**Why Did the British and Americans Bomb Dresden and Leipzig at the End of the War?**

In February 1945, as the Allied forces were closing in on the remnants of the Third Reich from all sides, American and British bombers dropped several tons of explosives on eastern German cities of Dresden and Leipzig. More than 30,000 civilians were killed in the Dresden bombings and another 2,000 Leipzig, although some accounts put the numbers much higher. The bombings were controversial at the time and remain so because they took place so close to the end of the war and the cities offered minimal strategic targets. Although there is no official British or American account that documents the reasons for those particular targets, it is believed that the bombings were intended to confuse the retreating German Army and to demoralize the German citizens in a similar effect that the atomic bombings of Hiroshima and Nagasaki later did.

## When Did the United Service Organizations Incorporated (USO) Form?

The USO is a non-profit organization that formed on February 4, 1941 to provide support for American military servicemen and their families and to raise morale among the troops. During World War II, the USO opened centers in most American cities that provided entertainment in the form of dances and vaudeville type live shows and also offered services for military members and their families. Perhaps the most famous legacy of the USO is the many "camp shows" it has put on at military bases, camps, and aboard ships overseas during wartime. Some famous American actors, such as Andy Rooney, were drafted into the military but did their service primarily in the USO. Hundreds of famous entertainers performed for American troops in both theaters of operations during World War II, including some of the following: Ed Sullivan, the Andrews Sisters, Barbara Stanwyck, Boris Karloff, Bing Crosby, and perhaps most notably, Bob Hope.

## What Was Operation Werewolf?

By late 1944 it appeared to many in the Nazi high command that their prospects of winning the war were slight to none and in all likelihood Germany would be overrun by both the Soviets and the Western Allies. Many Nazis began to believe that employing asymmetrical and guerilla tactics, as the

French Resistance and partisans had done to them, behind the lines would at least slow down the Allied advance, so *Unternehmen Werwolf* (Operation Werewolf) was instituted by Heinrich Himmler, the head of the SS. The origins of the name are unknown: it may have been derived from an early twentieth century novel; it was possibly a reference to Hitler, or it may have even been a reference to ancient Germanic legends of werewolves. The last reason is perhaps the most likely as the group's flag was a black banner with a white Germanic wolf's rune. Since the organization was secretive and was divided into autonomous cells, its numbers and long-range motives are difficult to gauge. It is known that members cached weapons, carried out assassinations of anti-Nazi officials, and conducted other acts of sabotage, but it is uncertain how long members intended to keep fighting. After the Nazis surrendered, though, Werewolf activities all but ceased.

## How Long Did the Battle of Berlin Last?

The Battle of Berlin, which was Nazi Germany's last stand against the Soviet Union, lasted took place from April 16 to May 2, 1945 for a total of two weeks and two days. With no more rivers or natural topography to slow down the Red Army, General Zhukov assembled three army groups totally nearly 2.5 million men and descended on the capital of the Third Reich. After pushing back what was left of the Wehrmacht forces just east of Berlin, the Red Army surrounded the capital and a siege ensued that was supported by American and British bombers. Fierce house to house fighting took place and the Germans were forced to enlist old men and young boys. Many German officers, such as General Kurt von Tippleskirch and SS Oberführer Felix Steiner, fought their way west to surrender to the Americans and British. General Helmuth Weidling and General Ferdinand

Schörner took their chances and surrendered to the Soviets, spending several years in Russian prisons. Still many other German commanders went down with the ship. Rear guard Red Army troops participated in numerous atrocities against the German population after the fighting was over.

## How Did Hitler Die?

Although there has been disagreements over the decades since his death, it is generally believed that Hitler killed himself with a single gunshot on April 10, 1945. As the Battle of Berlin raged and the Third Reich was about to collapse, Hitler and those closest to him waited in a bunker far below the Reich Chancellery for the inevitable. Eyewitnesses reported that Hitler killed himself with a single gunshot to the head, although he may have taken cyanide before the shot. His longtime girlfriend and wife of one day, Eva Braun, died of cyanide poisoning. Their bodies were taken to the surface and burned in order to prevent their desecration by the Soviets. The remains were later captured by the Soviets and moved several times, which led to several conspiracy theories of Hitler still being alive.

## When Was V-E Day?

V-E Day, or "Victory in Europe Day," which was the celebration of Germany's surrender in World War II, was originally held on May 8 and 9, 1945. May 8 was the day that hostilities ended, but May 9 was the day that Germany actually surrendered, which is why there are two days. Most of the western Allies originally marked May 8 as V-E day, while the Soviet Union and later the communist nations of eastern Europe celebrated May 9 as the end of the war where it became known as "Victory Day." May 8 saw millions of people take to the streets in celebration with some of the most memorable images coming from London's Piccadilly Circus and New York's Times Square.

# ON THE BATTLEFIELD: PACIFIC THEATER

### When Did the Battle of Midway Take Place?

The Battle of Midway took place from June 4 through June 7, 1942 on the Midway Atoll in the Pacific Ocean. The Japanese fleet, led by Admiral Yamamoto, hoped to draw out what was left of the American fleet from Hawaii. He reasoned that the American fleet would be defenseless without its land based aircraft, so the small American controlled Midway Atoll was chosen as the battle location. The Japanese miscalculated the size of the American fleet and the ability of the Americans to repair ships damaged during the Pearl Harbor attack, which meant that when the two fleets finally squared off they were of nearly equal size. American codebreakers were also able to ascertain the exact location of the Japanese fleet, which gave the Americans the element of surprise. The battle was a complete victory for the Americans—they sunk four Japanese carrier, shot down 248 Japanese aircraft, and killed more than 3,000 Japanese sailors. The Battle of Midway proved to be the turning point in the Pacific Theater as the Allies were on the offensive from that point forward.

### What Was the Island Hopping Strategy?

Geographically speaking, there were vast differences between the Pacific and European theaters in World War II. Unlike Germany, which is in the middle of the European continent, Japan is an archipelago/island nation that was far from any Allied bases and since the United States was doing the vast bulk of the fighting, defeating Japan involved traversing the vast expanse of the Pacific Ocean. In order to reach Japan, the United States military adopted the policy of island hopping or "leapfrogging," whereby small islands would be conquered in order to inch closer to Japan. In the process, some Japanese held islands deemed not strategic to the overall strategy were "hopped" or "leapfrogged."

## What Was the First Major Allied Offensive against the Japanese?

The Guadalcanal Campaign from August 7, 1942 to February 9, 1943 was the Allies first major offensive in the Pacific Theater of operations. The campaign took place in the Solomon Islands of the south Pacific and is named for the largest island in the chain and where the heaviest fighting took place, Guadalcanal. The long campaign was intended to stop the further advance of the Japanese and to deny them locations where they could build bases to bomb and/or potentially invade Australia and New Zealand. Logistically speaking, the campaign was quite complicated as it involved a large squadron of ships and planes along with more than 60,000 ground forces that had to be ferried from island to island as the Allies employed their island hopping strategy. The United States Marine Corps led the fight on land, as it did throughout most of the Pacific Theater, and contributed a fair amount of aircraft to the fight as well. The Japanese began an orderly in the middle of January and were off the Solomon Islands within a month.

## Who Used the First Intercontinental Weapon in World War II?

The Japanese used the first intercontinental weapons in history when they launched their Fu-Go fire balloons in late 1944 and early 1945. The Fu-Gos were unmanned hydrogen balloons that each carried an incendiary bomb intended to go off when the balloon crashed. The Fu-Go, like the V-2 in Germany, was a last ditch effort by the Japanese to turn the war by causing widespread destruction and havoc in North America. Over 9,000 of the balloons were launched, with some making it as far east as South Dakota, but did very little damage overall as they often landed in remote areas. A pregnant woman and five children in Oregon were the only fatalities from the Fu-Go attacks.

## How Did the *Raising the Flag on Iwo Jima* photograph Became so Iconic?

The Battle of Iwo Jima took place from February 19 to March 26, 1945 on the small volcanic island of Iwo Jima in the middle of the Pacific. The Japanese had heavily fortified the island because it was viewed by both sides as the last stop before Japan and because of that they fought nearly to the last man. When the battle was over, six American Marines – Rene Gagon, Ira Hayes, Harold Schultz, Michael Strank, Harlon Block, and Franklin Sousley – were photographed by Associated Press photographer Joe Rosenthal hoisting the American flag atop Mount Suribachi, which was actually the second flag raising that day. The photograph hit the wire and was reproduced in hundreds of newspapers across the United States. The image was later used for war propaganda and eventually became one of the most recognized images in American history. Rosenthal would win the 1945 Pulitzer Prize for Photography for the photo, further cementing it as one of the most memorable images from World War II.

## Were the Japanese Kamikazes Successful?

The world "kamikaze" is roughly translated into English from Japanese as "divine wind," was used to describe the Japanese pilots who flew their planes into Americans ships on suicide missions toward the end of the war in the Pacific. When the Japanese began losing island after island in the South Pacific, it became clear to their high command that something radical needed to be done in order to slow the American advance. Borrowing heavily from the medieval Japanese traditions of *bushido, seppuku*, and the samurai, the Japanese high command asked for volunteers to give their life for the state. The first kamikaze attacks took place during the Battle of Leyte Gulf (October 23-26, 1944) and continued until the end of the war. The exact numbers have been debated by historians from around the world, but it is estimated that around 19% of all kamikaze attacks hit their targets, sinking up to fifty American ships and killing approximately 5,000 sailors. Although the kamikaze attacks inflicted both material and psychological damage on the U.S. Navy, it was not enough for the Japanese to win the war.

## When Did President Roosevelt Die?

President Franklin D. Roosevelt died on April 12, 1945 from a cerebral hemorrhage in Warm Springs, Georgia at the age of sixty-three. Roosevelt's presidency was one of the most important in American history for a number of reasons. He led the country out of the Great Depression and through most of World War II, although his successor and Vice President, Harry Truman, saw the ultimate end of the war and its unraveling into the Cold War. Roosevelt was elected to an unprecedented four terms in office, which was due to a combination of his successful policies, luck, and his personable nature. He emphasized the last point in a number of ways, particularly with his "fire side chats," where he reassured the nation via radio speeches.

## What Was Operation Downfall?

Operation Downfall was the codename for the planned Allied invasion of Japan. Unlike Germany, which is located in the middle of continental Europe, Japan is an archipelago in the middle of the north Pacific, which would make any invasion logistically difficult and obvious with 1945 technology. By early 1945, though, it was becoming apparent to the Allies that the Japanese had no intention of surrendering: they fought almost to the last man in the small Pacific islands they held and had a large reserve of men willing to fight in Japan. The plan called for the invasion of Japan's most southerly island in early 1946, but it was called off when President Truman gave the order to drop the atomic/nuclear bombs on Hiroshima and Nagasaki.

## When Were Hiroshima and Nagasaki Bombed.

The two cities were bombed on August 6 and August 9, 1945 respectively. The first atomic/nuclear weapons had been developed by the scientists in the Manhattan Project, but President Truman only wanted to use them as a last resort. When it became apparent that the Japanese would not surrender unconditionally, President Truman gave the green light for the mission. The two cities were chosen because they were important ports for the Imperial Japanese Navy. The American B-29 bomber, *Enola Gay*, dropped the "Little Boy" bomb on Hiroshima and the American B-29 bomber, *Bockscar*, dropped the "Fat Man" bomb on Nagasaki. Both bombings left 250,000 Japanese military and civilians dead and forced the unconditional surrender of Emperor Hirohito.

## What Was Operation August Storm?

Operation August Storm is the name American historian David Glantz gave to the 1945 Soviet invasion of Manchuria in a 1983 academic paper. The invasion was significant for a few reasons: first, it began on August 9, just after the bombing of Hiroshima and hours before the bombing of Nagasaki. The second reason it was so important is because the Soviets and Japanese had not engaged in hostilities until that point, which lasted until August 20 and ended with a complete Soviet victory. The invasion helped force the Japanese into an unconditional surrender. Finally, the Soviet invasion established communism in North Korea and Mongolia and helped support Mao Zedong and his forces in China.

## When Was V-J Day?

Victory over Japan Day, usually known as "V-J Day," was actually on three different days: August 14, 1945; August 15, 1945; and September 2, 1945. The day represents Japan's surrender, which marked the official end of the Pacific Theater and World War II. The reason why there are three days is because the surrender took place on August 15 in Japan, but because of the time zone difference it was announced on August 14 in the United States. The September 2 date relates to the official surrender *ceremony* that was conducted on the *USS Missouri* in Tokyo Bay. Although September 2 is day recognized as the official V-J Day by the United States government, the celebrations captured on film and camera around the nation took place on August 14. In San Francisco, the partying turned to rioting with thirteen deaths, several rapes reported and several buildings were damaged and burned in bouts of looting and arson.

# CHAPTER 4:

# THE AFTERMATH OF THE WAR

## How Long Did the Nuremberg Trials Last?

The Nuremberg trials were a number of different trials held by the Allies against various members of the Axis powers, especially high-ranking Nazis, for war crimes and crimes against humanity. The trials lasted from November 20, 1945 until October 1, 1946 in the city of Nuremberg, Germany. The site was chosen because it was largely undamaged from the war and it was also the location of early Nazi Party rallies. More than 200 men were tried for a variety of crimes and received sentences ranging from ten years in prison to death. Some, such as architect Albert Speer, who received a twenty year sentence, expressed repentance, while others, such as theorist Alfred Rosenberg, were defiant until their executions.

## How Long Did the Tokyo Trial Last?

The International Military Tribunal for the Far East, or more commonly known as the "Tokyo Trial," was essentially the Pacific version of the Nuremberg Trials, where high ranking members of the Japanese military and government were tried for crimes against humanity. As opposed to the high number of officials who were tried at Nuremberg, only twenty-eight Japanese officials stood trial in Tokyo and also unlike

Nuremberg, the proceedings in Tokyo only lasted one day, April 29, 1946. Seven of the defendants, including Hideki Tojo, were sentenced to death by hanging, which were carried out at the Sugamo Prison on December 23, 1948.

## Did More Americans Die in the European or Pacific Theater of War?

Overall, 405,399 Americans were killed in action during World War II with around 161,000 American deaths either on the battlefield or as the result of combat in the Pacific Theater and 244,399 in the European Theater. Although more American servicemen died in the European Theater, the fighting in the Pacific was often more brutal. There were also more troops sent to Europe as the American government's policy during the war was "Europe First."

## What Country Suffered the Most Loses in World War II?

Without a doubt, the Soviet Union suffered far more losses than any country in every category. The Germans destroyed 70,000 Soviet villages and 1,700 cities, killing up to 20 million civilians. The number of Soviet military personnel was around eight million, which even if the numbers were exaggerated by Stalin and the Communist Party as some historians have suggested, put the Soviet losses far ahead of any other country. The brutality that the Germans often inflicted on the Russians was repaid by the Red Army when it conquered eastern Germany and killed and raped thousands of civilians.

## Who Was Represented at the Yalta Conference?

The Yalta Conference was hosted by Joseph Stalin and the Soviet Union in the Soviet city of Yalta from February 4 to 11, 1945. The three major Allied leaders were in attendance – American President Franklin Roosevelt, British Prime

Minister Winston Churchill, and Soviet Premier Joseph Stalin– to ultimately decide the fate of post-war Europe. Some of the basic features were worked out at Yalta, such as the partition and occupation of Germany, but details had to be worked out in later conferences and agreements.

## When Was the Potsdam Conference Held?

The Potsdam Conference, held Potsdam, Germany, took place from July 17 to August 2, 1945. After Germany was defeated on the battlefield and agreed to an unconditional surrender, the "Big Three" leaders of Stalin, Churchill, and Truman, who had become American President upon Roosevelt's death, met once more to discuss the fate of post-war Europe. Churchill was joined by Clement Attlee, who had just become the new British Prime Minister after a July 5 general election. The victors came to general agreements on the continued military occupation of Germany and the prosecution of Nazis for war crimes, but clear fault lines emerged between the Soviets and Americans.

## When Was Germany Split into West and East Germany?

Germany was partitioned into democratic-capitalist West Germany (Federal German Republic) and Marxist-communist East Germany (German Democratic Republic) in 1949. Germany was immediately occupied by the Allies after World War II with each of the major powers getting zones of influence under the terms of the Potsdam Conference. As tensions between the Soviet Union and the Western powers began to build, West Germany was established as a country on May 23, 1949 with its capital in the otherwise unnoteworthy city of Bonn. The communists responding by establishing East Germany on October 7, 1949 with East Berlin as its capital.

## Was "De-Nazification" Effective?

Before Germany was defeated, the Western Allies realized that military success would only be half the victory—they believed that German society needed to be fundamentally transformed and rid of any Nazi influences in order to achieve true victory. In order to achieve this goal, the Allies embarked on an ambitious program, termed "De-Nazification," which targeted all aspects of Nazi Germany for removal. At the most mundane level, all symbols of Nazism were physically removed, but the entire system was overhauled: members of the Nazi Party were assessed of their guilt, the media was retooled to promote anti-Nazi propaganda, and the idea of German collective guilt for the war in general and the Holocaust specifically was disseminated in schools and the press. The limits of De-Nazification, though, were manifested when the Cold War began. Both the Western Allies and the Soviets quickly placed former Nazis with military and administrative experience into the militaries and governments of West and East Germany and both sides grabbed as many Nazi rocket scientists they could for their nascent space programs.

## Who Was Hans-Ulrich Rudel

Hans-Ulrich Rudel (1916-1982) was an ace Stuka pilot in the Luftwaffe during World War II and Neo-Nazi organizer after the war. During the war, Rudel flew more than 2,5000 missions on the Eastern Front, destroying over 500 tanks, more than 150 artillery pieces, a battleship, a cruiser, and seven other aircraft despite Stukas being woefully armed for air combat. Rudel was highly decorated for his service and received awards from Hitler personally. He surrendered to the Americans at the end of the war and was released after a year because he was not a member of the Nazi Party and did not face any war crimes charges. Rudel moved to Argentina in 1948 and established close ties within the militaries and right-wing governments of southern South America, using his connections to aid fugitive Nazis. While in Argentina, Rudel wrote books and articles about his time in World War II and his political ideas, bringing together a new, global Neo-Nazi movement with surviving Nazis. Because he was never wanted for any war crimes, Rudel was able to move about the world openly, eventually retiring to and dying in West Germany.

## Where is Mussolini's Tomb?

Benito Mussolini's tomb is located in his family's crypt in Predappio, Italy. Unlike Germany, where any positive, non-academic portrayal of the Third Reich is subject to prosecution, the Allies and the post-war Italian government took a much more lenient view towards Fascist Italy. As a result, Mussolini's tomb has become a focal point for neo-Nazi and neo-Fascist groups from around the world. The anniversary of Mussolini's execution draws thousands of neo-Fascists every year, where they march through the small northern Italian town carrying flags and giving the Fascist/Nazi/Roman salute, which is legal in Italy but banned in Germany.

## What Happened to Displaced Peoples after the War?

The general social upheaval of the war created a mass of migrations and changes to national boarders, especially in Europe. Many of the Jewish survivors of Nazi Germany made their way to the United States but even more went to Palestine. The tremendous increase in the number of Jews in Palestine led to the formation of the Jewish state of Israel on May 14, 1948. Most Axis soldiers were at least temporarily held in POW camps after the war and if they were deemed to not be a threat they were allowed to return to their homes, if they still existed. For the most part, the national borders in western Europe went back to what they were before the war, but the situation was far different in eastern Europe. Stalin quickly gobbled up the Baltic states and incorporated them into the Soviet Union, which began about a decade long series of forced migrations of millions of people. Ethnic Germans who were living in Hungary, Romania, Poland, and the Balkans were forced to move to West or East Germany, even if they no longer had contacts in either country. Finns living in the Soviet occupied region around Lake Ladoga had to migrate to Finland, Baltic peoples were moved into Russia, and ethnic Russians were sent to the Baltic republics.

## What Happened to Königsberg?

Since Königsberg was located in the so-called "Polish Corridor," it was separated from Germany proper. It was a heavily protected German city and became the site of some of the fiercest German resistance during World War II. When the city finally fell to the Red Army on April 9, 1945, most of the remaining German civilians were either massacred in reprisals or sent to work in labor camps for several years. Per the Allied agreement at Potsdam, the Königsberg and the region around it became part of the Soviet Union, the name of the city was changed to Kaliningrad, and most signs of its German background were eliminated.

## When Was the State of Israel Founded?

The Jewish state of Israel was founded on May 14, 1948. A combination of a vast influx of Jewish migrants from Europe and public sympathy for the Jewish people in the West in the wake of World War II led to the newly formed United Nations supporting the idea, but the Jewish community in

Palestine, led by David Ben-Gurion, proclaimed the state the day before British control of Palestine expired.

## When Did the Marshall Plan Go into Effect?

The Foreign Assistance Act of 1948, otherwise known as the Marshall Plan, became effective on April 3, 1948 and in July the aid began going to the nations in western Europe hardest hit by World War II. The plan, which was largely the idea of Secretary of State George Marshall, therefore the name, was to primarily rebuild Europe after the war, but also to provide a bulwark against the spread of communism. The Act passed through both houses of Congress with support from both parties and was signed into law by President Harry Truman, who believed that it would play a key role in his anti-communist doctrine. Joseph Stalin felt that the Marshall Plan was a ploy by the United States to gain leverage over the countries of Europe, so he opposed the plan and pressured the leaders of the new communist states in eastern Europe to do the same. Approximately $13.5 billion in the form of grants was disbursed to western Europe from 1948 to 1951.

## What Was the Cominform?

Cominform, short for "Communist Information Bureau," was the international umbrella organization of all the communist governments in the world and the major communist parties in France and Italy. It was formed on October 5, 1947, ostensibly as a united front against the West among the countries that refused the Marshall Plan, but in reality was a vehicle by which the Soviets could keep a close eye on the new communist states of eastern Europe. One of Cominform's missions was the coordinate economic assistance to communist countries affected by World War II, similar in purpose to the Marshall Plan.

## What Happened to Soviet Prisoners of War after They Came Home?

When the war was finally over, most POWs on both sides were glad to return home, but there were exceptions. Some of the high-ranking members of the Nazi Party, German military, and Japanese military were tried for war crimes and many Red Army POWs faced uncertain fates after they returned to the Soviet Union. Most Soviet POWs were accused by the Stalin regime of being infected with fascist ideas and sent to labor in the Soviet Union's many gulags alongside political prisoners and common criminals. The most famous Soviet POW to be sent to a gulag after the war was Aleksandr Solzhenitsyn, who wrote about his travails in the *Gulag Archipelago* and *A Day in the Life of Ivan Denisovich*. After Stalin died in 1953 most of the Soviet POWs serving time in gulags were released, finally ending the war for them.

## When Did the Cold War Begin?

Most historians generally assign 1946 as the beginning of the Cold War. When the three major Allied nations met at Yalta and Potsdam to discuss post-war Europe, it was obvious that the United States and the United Kingdom had a far different vision than Stalin and the Soviet Union. After the Soviet Union created communist pro-Soviet puppet states throughout eastern Europe, many Western leaders began seeing their former ally as a new enemy. This view was best articulated by Winston Churchill in his "Sinews of Peace" speech delivered at Westminster College in Fulton, Missouri on March 5, 1946. In that speech, Churchill famously proclaimed that "an iron curtain has descended across the Continent." American President Harry Truman proclaimed the anti-communist Truman Doctrine in 1947 and the Berlin Blockade took place in 1948, which was a point of no going back for U.S-U.S.S.R. relations.

## Why Did so Many Nazis Go to Argentina after World War II?

After the war, several former Nazis and high ranking German military officials who were facing lengthy prison or death sentences for war crimes decided that they would be safer in countries that were not cooperating with the international tribunals. Initially many went to Spain where General Franco gave them safe passage and from there most went either to the Middle East or South America. Argentina became a particularly attractive place for many of them to go due to the country's culture and political situation. Unlike many other Latin American countries, Argentina had a very small Indian population, imported very few African slaves, and experienced high levels of European immigration in the late nineteenth century that was similar to the United States. Most of the immigrants were from Italy and Spain, but there were also a large number of Germans, many of whom kept ties with the Old World. Besides Argentina's European culture and temperate climate, Juan Perón was the country's president from 1944 to September 1955. Perón was a populist with fascist sympathies who openly gave asylum to Nazis, especially ones that could aid his government's military and intelligence services. Some of the more notable Nazis who made Argentina their home after the war were Erik Priebke, Josef Mengele, and Adolf Eichmann, who were notably extracted from Argentina by Israeli Mossad agents in 1960. Later, fugitive Nazis also found sanctuary in the right-wing military dictatorships of Chile, Paraguay, and Brazil.

## Why Did Nazis Go to the Middle East after the War?

South American was not the only destination for former Nazis, many started new lives in Syria and Egypt, where they were free from prosecution. The most famous Nazi who fled to the Middle East after the war was Alois Brunner, who was convicted of numerous crimes against humanity *in absentia*. Brunner died in Syria, in either 2001 or 2010, as one of the highest ranking Nazis never to have been prosecuted. Former Nazis were given asylum in Syria by dictator Hafez al-Asad and later in Egypt by Gamal Nasser in hopes that they would help modernize their military and intelligence agencies in their fight against the newly created Jewish state of Israel.

## Was ODESSA Real?

The existence of ODESSA—*Organisation der ehemaligen SS-Angehörigen* (English: Organization of Former SS Members)—has been argued by academics, military members, and intelligence officials since the end of World War II. The term actually originated with American intelligence agencies as a codename for their hunt for former Nazis. Simon Wiesnthal argued that the organization existed and pointed to the hundreds of high ranking Nazis that made it safely to the Middle East and South America after the war was proof. Today, though, most academics argue that the lack of documentary evidence argues against its existence and that no such organization was needed when the Nazis had sympathetic dictators who would protect them, namely: Franco, Assad, Nasser, Perón, Stroessner, and Pinochet.

## What Is the Origin of the Term "Holocaust"

The word "holocaust" is derived from Greek word *holocaustos*, meaning "burnt offering." It is believed to have first been used to describe a modern genocide in reference to Turkish massacres of Armenians in the late eighteenth and early twentieth centuries. Jews usually referred to the Nazi genocide of European Jewry by the Hebrew word *shoah*. The term "holocaust" began to specifically refer to the attempted genocide of European Jewry during World War II in the late 1970s in the United States when it was used in the television mini-series, *Holocaust*.

**Who Was Kurt Waldheim?**

Kurt Waldheim (1918-2007) was a former Nazi and soldier in the Wehrmacht who became the Fourth Secretary General of the United Nations (1972-1981) and President of Austria (1986-1992). Waldheim was born in Austria but became involved with the Nazi Party after Austria was annexed in 1938. He served in the Wehrmacht during World War II, primarily on the Eastern Front and in the Balkans and Greece. After the war, Waldheim rose in both Austrian and international politics, but his service in World War II constantly followed him. Famed Nazi hunter Simon Wiesenthal and members of the World Jewish Congress alleged that he misrepresented his complicity in war crimes, but Waldheim and his supporters, which included Pope John Paul II, argued that he knew little about atrocities being committed and what he did know he was unable to stop. In 1987, the United States government announced that it had evidence linking Waldheim to war crimes and that he would be barred entry into the country, despite being a head of state.

**When Was the Office of Special Investigations Established?**

The Office of Special Investigations (OSI), which is a unit within the United States Justice Department, was established in 1979 with the primary intention of identifying former Nazis and other war criminals from World War II who were living in the United States. The OSI would then refer certain cases to the Justice Department for either prosecution and/or deportation. Perhaps the most high-profile case the OSI was involved in and which brought it the most attention was that of John Demajanjuk. Demajanjuk was a Ukrainian immigrant who immigrated to the United States after World War II and worked in an auto plant in Ohio. Demajanjuk was identified as a Nazi collaborator and a concentration camp guard in the late 1970s and was deported to Israel in 1986 to stand trial for war crimes. Despite being acquitted by the Israeli courts of war crimes in 1993 and sent back to the United States, was stripped of his citizenship and deported to Germany in 2009. Today, since most former Nazis are now dead, the OSI's mission is to identify other foreign human rights violators living in the United States.

## When Was the Last Confirmed Japanese "Holdout" Captured?

Teuro Nakamura (1919-1979), a Taiwan born Imperial Japanese soldier of Amis ethnicity, was discovered in a remoted location of Indonesia in mid-1974 and arrested by Indonesian soldiers on December 18, 1974 and is the last known "holdout." The holdouts were Japanese soldiers who either refused to surrender when their country did in 1945, or simply did not know the war was over because they were stranded on remote South Pacific islands. Dozens of holdouts emerged from the jungles of Indonesia and remote islands in the Pacific during the 1940s to turn themselves into authorities, but the numbers began to drastically decline in the 1950s and 1960s as surviving in such isolated locations is extremely difficult, even for men accustomed to austerity. Although Nakamura was the last confirmed holdout captured, Shigeyuki Hashimoto and Kiyoaki Tanaka returned to Japan from Malaysia in 1990. The two men were fighting in Malaysia when the war ended and decided to stay and later joined the Malayan Communist Party's insurgency, so it is questionable if Hashimoto and Tanaka were true holdouts.

Reports of holdouts continued well into the 1990s but no evidence exists of any holdouts living past 1980. The holdout phenomenon was parodied in a 1965 episode of *Gilligan's Island*, where a holdout held the castaways as his prisoner.

# DON'T FORGET YOUR FREE BOOKS

# MORE BOOKS BY BILL O'NEILL

I hope you enjoyed this book and learned something new. Please feel free to check out some of my previous books on **Amazon.**

Printed in Poland
by Amazon Fulfillment
Poland Sp. z o.o., Wrocław

50467064R00067